"These tools are very useful. I can imagine using many of them in my role PARENT'S SHELF
as CCSS facilitator. I wish I'd had this book a year ago!"
—Kim Rensch, Middle Level CCSS facilitator, Fargo Public Schools

The Common Sense Guide to the Common Core

Teacher-Tested Tools — DIGITAL CONTENT CONTAINS OVER **300 PAGES** OF FILL-IN STANDARDS MATRICES — for Implementation

Katherine McKnight, Ph.D.

free spirit
PUBLISHING®

Library of Congress Cataloging-in-Publication Data
McKnight, Katherine.
    The common sense guide to the Common Core : teacher-tested tools for implementation / Katherine McKnight.
            pages cm
        Includes bibliographical references and index.
    ISBN 978-1-57542-468-2 (paperback) — ISBN 1-57542-468-1 1. Education—Standards—United States—States. 2. Education—Curricula—Standards—United States—States. I. Title.
    LB3060.83.M3796 2014
    379.1'58—dc23
                                                                        2014000227

eBook ISBN: 978-1-57542-592-4

Edited by Meg Bratsch
Cover and interior design by Tasha Kenyon
Compass image © Mailis Laos | Dreamstime.com

10 9 8 7 6 5 4 3 2 1
Printed in the United States of America

Free Spirit Publishing Inc.
Minneapolis, MN
(612) 338-2068
help4kids@freespirit.com
www.freespirit.com

DEDICATION

For Jim, Ellie, and Colin, who bring joy to my life.

ACKNOWLEDGMENTS

When the Common Core State Standards (CCSS) were first published in 2010 I was ambivalent. I am not a fan of the first generation of standards that were created during the No Child Left Behind (NCLB) decade. During NCLB I witnessed an obsession with testing and compliance; it was a prescriptive period. I am, however, an avid supporter of the CCSS, because they provide a coherent structure in which educators can create curriculum and instruction that meets the contextual needs of students. It is classroom teachers, and the administrators who support their work in the classroom, who create engaging learning environments for students.

I want to thank all of the teachers I have met in professional development workshops and schools all over the United States who are passionate about teaching and learning. My teacher colleagues are my muses, and I wrote this book for them.

The Free Spirit Publishing team made this book possible. I am grateful for their vision, and I'm especially grateful to Meg Bratsch for her outstanding editing and "awesomeness." Speaking of awesome, my family Jim, Ellie, and Colin are always supportive of my work and are my greatest cheerleaders. I also want to thank Anna Johnson, Kris Lantzy, and Elaine Carlson, who keep me organized and provide great ideas for representing my work. Finally, I want to acknowledge my mom, Patricia Siewert (1934–2008), a Chicago Public School teacher for more than thirty-five years. I still hear her whispering her mantra to me: "Teaching is an act of love and social justice."

Contents

LIST OF FIGURES

LIST OF REPRODUCIBLE PAGES

Download these forms at **freespirit.com/CSG2CC-forms**. Use the password **4etools**.

DIGITAL DOWNLOAD CONTENTS

Download these forms at **freespirit.com/CSG2CC-forms**. Use the password **4etools**.

Forms from the Book (see List of Reproducible Pages on pages vii–viii)

Bonus Materials (*denotes forms that are also included in the Appendix of this book)

TOOL #18: THE CCSS ELA GRADES K–12 MATRICES

Kindergarten English Language Arts Common Core State Standards

Grade 1 English Language Arts Common Core State Standards

Grade 2 English Language Arts Common Core State Standards

Grade 3 English Language Arts Common Core State Standards*

Grade 4 English Language Arts Common Core State Standards*

Grade 5 English Language Arts Common Core State Standards*

Grade 6 English Language Arts Common Core State Standards*

Grade 7 English Language Arts Common Core State Standards*

Grade 8 English Language Arts Common Core State Standards*

Grades 9–10 English Language Arts Common Core State Standards

Grades 11–12 English Language Arts Common Core State Standards

Grades 6–8 Writing Common Core State Standards

Grades 9–10 Writing Common Core State Standards

Grades 11–12 Writing Common Core State Standards

TOOL #19: THE CCSS INTERDISCIPLINARY LITERACY GRADES 6–12 MATRICES

Grades 6–8 History and Social Studies Common Core State Standards

Grades 6–8 Science and Technical Subjects Common Core State Standards

Grades 9–10 History and Social Studies Common Core State Standards

Grades 9–10 Science and Technical Subjects Common Core State Standards

Grades 11–12 History and Social Studies Common Core State Standards

Grades 11–12 Science and Technical Subjects Common Core State Standards

TOOL #20: THE CCSS MATH GRADES K–12 MATRICES

Kindergarten English Language Arts Common Core State Standards

Grade 1 Math Common Core State Standards

Grade 2 Math Language Arts Common Core State Standards

Grade 3 Math Language Arts Common Core State Standards

Grade 4 Math Language Arts Common Core State Standards

Grade 5 Math Language Arts Common Core State Standards

Grade 6 Math Language Arts Common Core State Standards

Grade 7 Math Language Arts Common Core State Standards

Grade 8 Math Language Arts Common Core State Standards

Grades 9–12 Number and Quantity Common Core State Standards

Grades 9–12 Algebra Common Core State Standards

Grades 9–12 Functions Common Core State Standards

Grades 9–12 Geometry Common Core State Standards

Grades 9–12 Statistics and Probability Common Core State Standards

Introduction

When the Common Core State Standards (CCSS) were first introduced in 2010, I thought, "Good grief! Here we go again." I'll be blunt: I disliked the state standards that were instituted, partially, in response to No Child Left Behind. These state-based standards and assessments left many of us with long lists of expectations that were fixed on the lowest rank of Bloom's Taxonomy—the knowledge, or recall, level. Not surprisingly, after more than a decade of using this framework we find the nation's students largely unprepared for the demands of college and twenty-first-century careers.

Nevertheless, I had to reevaluate the validity of the Common Core when I discovered on page four of the CCSS document something to convince me that the Common Core standards were different:

> *Teachers are thus free to provide students with whatever tools and knowledge their professional judgment and experience identify as most helpful for meeting the goals set out in the Standards.*

There it was, in black and white. Educators—teachers and curriculum specialists—were being credited for their judgment, experience, and skills. *Teachers,* not policymakers, were charged with identifying the most appropriate methods for meeting goals. While this approach may seem like common sense, it was something that I hadn't heard in years.

The CCSS framework, adopted by all but four states as of January 2014, offers a coherent paradigm that helps teachers develop effective classroom environments. In these classrooms, all students will be able to receive the high level of instruction needed to prepare them for the future.

Three key features of the CCSS raise the expectations placed on students:

1. **Literacy.** Literacy is a foundational feature of the Common Core. The authors of the CCSS promote the idea that if students are to be college and career ready, they must understand a variety of challenging texts. Further, to facilitate this goal, literacy skills must be taught by teachers of all content areas, not just English language arts. The literacy standards are divided into four strands: reading, writing, speaking and listening, and language.

2. **Reading complexity.** The College and Career Readiness Anchor Standards for reading are divided into three areas: key ideas and details, craft and structure, and integration of knowledge and ideas. Within each area, students are expected to achieve certain levels of reading complexity and comprehension in order to be ready for college or careers.

3. **Conceptual understanding.** The mathematics standards promote conceptual understanding as well as procedural skill. It's not enough for students to solve equations; they must take the information and apply it on a conceptual level.

The CCSS represent a significant challenge for educators and schools. The standards demand that we shift from merely conveying information. Instead, we are now free to engage students in the more sophisticated thought processes of analysis and synthesis.

KEY ELEMENTS OF THE COMMON CORE

The Common Core State Standards were written in response to the first round of standards, developed in the 1990s by individual states. Assessments that measure this early round of state-specific standards have made it difficult to compare students across the country. The National Assessment of Educational Progress (NAEP) has been our only reliable, nationwide measure of student achievement. During the past decade, NAEP results have revealed substantial differences among states in all content areas—but particularly in literacy. The CCSS address this problem by providing educators with not only a coherent set of expectations for literacy skill development (and other content areas), but also a more uniform understanding of student performance and academic achievement. In addition, the standards and assessments are intended to create a common language among educators that will, in turn, lead to shared conversation and a common commitment to preparing students for college and careers. The following eight key elements form the main focus areas of the CCSS:

1. High-level comprehension

2. Challenging texts, with greater emphasis on informational texts

3. Technology-based resources

4. Expository and argumentative writing

5. Oral language skills (speaking and listening)

6. Academic language and vocabulary

7. College and career readiness

8. Literacy skills in *all* content areas

The Common Core State Standards increase the expectations for student literary achievement in various ways. The central focus of the new standards is ***comprehension***. For students to be college and career ready, they must be able to understand a wide variety of challenging texts. Students are expected to engage in careful reading of both main ideas and details, perceiving how the information is organized, recognizing and evaluating the author's craft, synthesizing a variety of texts, and responding critically to these texts. These are all high-level comprehension skills.

The CCSS also establish an expectation that students will read more difficult texts than they currently do. This is in response to NAEP data that indicates more than 60 percent of students are not proficient readers. In order for students to develop high-level reading skills, they must engage in reading ***complex yet accessible texts.*** Differentiated texts and increased content-area reading are essential as we position students to meet these more rigorous expectations.

The Common Core State Standards pay significantly greater attention to informational texts than did previous generations of standards. With the greater focus on informational texts, we now have a broader range of materials that can develop literacy skills in diverse content areas. When students read a wide variety of texts that includes a strong focus on *informational texts,* they are developing their skills in reading to build knowledge.

The CCSS also recognize that the ways in which information is communicated in the twenty-first century is dramatically new and different. Students are expected to use a range of digital resources, visual and graphic information, and other *technology-based resources* to build their knowledge. And these resources are to be used not only for gathering new information, but also for presenting this information to others.

To support students' acquisition of presentation skills, the Common Core writing standards represent a dramatic shift from extensive personal narratives to *expository and argumentative writing.* Students are expected to glean vast knowledge through encounters with a full array of texts. Then they are expected to represent what they know and understand through writing.

Speaking and listening are oftentimes referred to as neglected or forgotten literacies. In contrast, the CCSS embrace the value of *oral language.* Like reading and writing, speaking and listening are literacies that enable students to gather new information and present what they know and understand.

The CCSS also include a language strand that widens the scope beyond a focus on mechanics. The language strand incorporates expectations for *academic language and vocabulary* in both written and oral communication, while also covering grammar and usage conventions and knowledge of how language functions in different contexts.

As we transition to the CCSS we must remember that the emphasis is on skill building for *college and career readiness.* Our twenty-first-century students can gather information from a staggering number of sources, but they still need to learn how to use this information. The literacy skills they develop in school should provide the means to do so.

A core element of CCSS that helps students prepare for college and career readiness is building literacy skills in *all content areas.* The new CCSS-based assessments developed by the Partnership for the Assessment of Readiness for College and Careers (PARCC) and by the Smarter Balanced Assessment Consortium require broad literacy skills that are not exclusive to English language arts (ELA). Literacy skills are the responsibility of all teachers, not just the English language arts teachers. This is why the ELA standards include interdisciplinary literacy standards. When I work with teachers all over the country in examining the assessment examples from PARCC and from Smarter Balanced, math teachers are quick to point out that the students who do not have excellent reading skills will be unable to respond to the more complex and application-based problems that are now the norm for CCSS assessments.

MYTHS AND REALITIES SURROUNDING THE COMMON CORE STATE STANDARDS

Since the CCSS were introduced in 2010, I have encountered many rumors and mis-understandings about these new standards. I'd like to set the record straight regarding some of the myths.

Myth #1: The CCSS were a federal mandate.

Actually, the Common Core State Standards initiative is a state-led effort coordinated jointly by the National Governors Association Center for Best Practices and by the Council of Chief State School Officers.

Myth #2: Educators were not involved in the development of the CCSS.

That's not true. The standards were developed in collaboration with teachers, school administrators, and experts to provide a clear and consistent framework to prepare students for college and careers.

Myth #3: The CCSS do not address the needs of students with special needs.

Well, I can see how this rumor got started. In the introduction of the CCSS document, the authors indicate that it is teachers and curriculum specialists who know best how students can develop the skills articulated in the new standards. Therefore, the document does not include recommendations for students with special needs. Nor do the standards recommend specific curriculum or instructional methodologies. Instead, individual school districts and states are given the freedom to determine how to best meet the needs of students with special needs.

Myth #4: The CCSS do little to address the achievement gap.

The CCSS place the trust in teachers and curriculum specialists to make instructional decisions. Specific strategies or methods are not listed in the CCSS, because they are based on the professional reality that educators are in the best position to know what will actually work to meet the instructional needs and achievement gaps of the students in a given classroom. The CCSS emphasize results rather than means. As such, their purpose is to lay out the expectations and skills needed for college and career readiness, not the curriculum and instructional means by which these expectations are met.

Myth #5: With all of the focus on college and career readiness, the CCSS ignore the immediate developmental needs of students.

Similar to my response to Myth #4, the CCSS emphasize that educators, not policy-makers, know best how to develop the skills that are articulated in the standards. The transition to the Common Core State Standards and their rigorous expectations is a process that takes time to implement. The anchor standards and grade-level articulations are vertically and horizontally aligned, which means that students at different ability levels are working on the same skill but at different levels of competency. Thus, instruction must meet the current needs of students.

Myth #6: Differentiated instruction is mandated by the CCSS.

Again, the CCSS authors do not mandate or make suggestions for any particular curriculum or instructional methodology. Why? The CCSS recognize, quite emphatically, that it is teachers and curriculum specialists who are the most knowledgeable about the abilities of students in any given educational context.

Myth #7: We aren't allowed to teach literature anymore.

This is not true. In the CCSS Appendices, the authors clearly explain that there should be a *balance* between literature and informational text. Of all the myths I encounter, I find this one the most frustrating. The role of informational text in the CCSS English language arts curriculum is so misunderstood that I feel compelled to address it further.

Literary Nonfiction vs. Informational Texts

The CCSS are based on recommendations from the National Reading Panel that are rooted in research. For the ELA standards, informational texts are defined as "literary nonfiction," which can include biographies, memoirs, letters, speeches, or diaries. For all other content areas, informational texts include textbooks, blogs, news articles, and other reference materials. This distinction is critical, and is illustrated in the following excerpt from the CCSS ELA document:

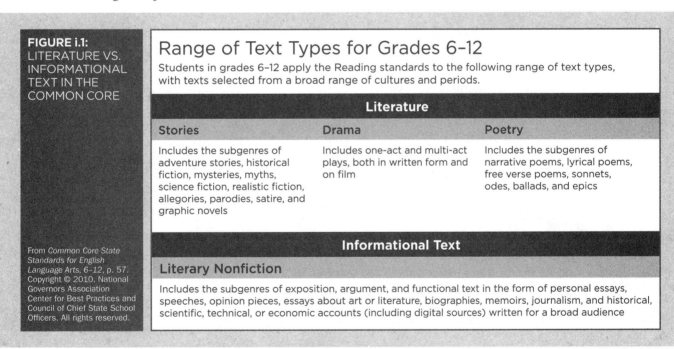

FIGURE i.1: LITERATURE VS. INFORMATIONAL TEXT IN THE COMMON CORE

Range of Text Types for Grades 6–12

Students in grades 6–12 apply the Reading standards to the following range of text types, with texts selected from a broad range of cultures and periods.

Literature

Stories	Drama	Poetry
Includes the subgenres of adventure stories, historical fiction, mysteries, myths, science fiction, realistic fiction, allegories, parodies, satire, and graphic novels	Includes one-act and multi-act plays, both in written form and on film	Includes the subgenres of narrative poems, lyrical poems, free verse poems, sonnets, odes, ballads, and epics

Informational Text

Literary Nonfiction

Includes the subgenres of exposition, argument, and functional text in the form of personal essays, speeches, opinion pieces, essays about art or literature, biographies, memoirs, journalism, and historical, scientific, technical, or economic accounts (including digital sources) written for a broad audience

As we consider the role of informational text, it must be within the context of the entire school curriculum, *including all content areas other than English language arts*. For example, when we discuss percentages of literature and informational text to be read at each grade level, we're talking about all classes in a schoolwide curriculum. English language arts is just one of many courses. Literature (both fiction and literary nonfiction) is still, and always will be, the primary emphasis in an English language arts course. From a reading instructional perspective, literature helps students develop high-level comprehension skills because of its inferential meanings, figurative language, and linguistic complexity. Informational texts (excluding literary nonfiction) characteristically do not contain these features. Therefore, while some informational texts are still read in ELA courses, they also need to be read in courses other than ELA.

The point of the CCSS reading framework is best summarized in Reading Anchor Standard 10, in which students are expected to *"read and comprehend complex literary and informational texts independently and proficiently."* The reading standards are not so much about percentages of literature and informational text within the curriculum, but rather about increasing the overall amount of reading.

ABOUT THIS BOOK

Now that we've addressed the "why" of the new standards, their construction, and what they mean for students, we need to address the "how." How can teachers meet the expectations for skill development called for in the new standards? There is no quick answer to this question; I'll begin with some background.

My first experience working with teachers transitioning to CCSS was back in 2011. At that time, few educators were aware of the paradigm shifts created by the CCSS and what it would mean for teachers and students. As we designed a curriculum aligned to the new CCSS for mathematics and English language arts, we included research-based methods in our plans to teach the new curriculum. Some of the methods we used included project-based learning, learning centers, reader's workshop, and writer's workshop. As we dug deeply into the new standards, we discovered that students must work at the highest levels on Bloom's Taxonomy in order to develop content knowledge and literacy skills (see **Figure i.2**). As you examine the standards, you'll notice high-level skills such as analysis, synthesis, comparing and contrasting, and representation. These carefully worded expectations transition students to the highest level of knowledge and understanding.

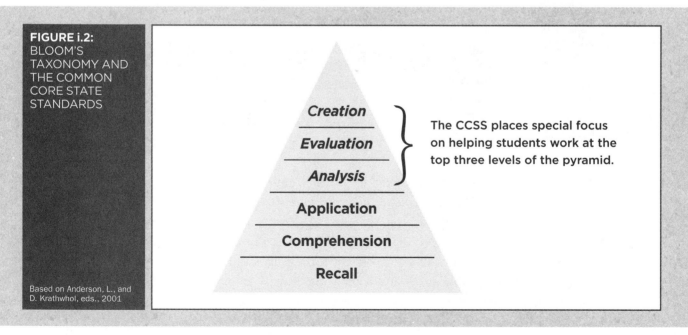

FIGURE i.2:
BLOOM'S TAXONOMY AND THE COMMON CORE STATE STANDARDS

Creation
Evaluation
Analysis
Application
Comprehension
Recall

The CCSS places special focus on helping students work at the top three levels of the pyramid.

Based on Anderson, L., and D. Krathwhol, eds., 2001

After creating a math and ELA curriculum aligned with CCSS, I worked further with educators to develop a set of tools that would support teachers as they gain an understanding of the new standards. Most of the tools were fleshed out during professional development days, or during sustained professional learning communities (PLCs)—those regular meetings that give teachers the opportunity to work together to build professional knowledge. Since 2011, these tools have been used by thousands of teachers and school administrators throughout the United States. They have been used successfully in a wide variety of educational contexts. Each tool has been revised as a result of substantial teacher feedback. This book became a reality in response to many teacher requests for its publication.

The Common Sense Guide to the Common Core contains forty tools designed to help teachers, administrators, and their colleagues develop a plan for implementing the new standards. Each tool is described in depth; often it is accompanied by a figure of the tool filled in with sample text or labeled with annotations. The tools themselves are presented as full-page graphic organizers following the tool description and example tool, if applicable. They can be duplicated, filled in on the page, or printed from the digital download for use in professional development and curriculum planning groups. (See page ix for instructions on how to access the digital download.) The following paragraphs summarize the content and tools addressed in each chapter of this book.

Chapter 1: Understanding the Common Core State Standards. The starting point for transitioning to the CCSS is a thorough reading of the document. The tools in Chapter 1 are packed with important information and resources that will support you and your colleagues as you transition to the new standards.

Chapter 2: Analyzing Your Current Standards and Curriculum. The best advice I have ever heard an educator share with colleagues as they prepare to embark on CCSS implementation is: "Don't throw out your current curriculum!" You probably already have instructional practices in place that are Common Core aligned. The tools in this chapter will guide you through a thorough study and audit of your current curriculum as you and your colleagues identify areas that may need revision for CCSS alignment.

Chapter 3: Transitioning to the Common Core. Any transition requires a great plan. The tools in this chapter focus on building curriculum that develops the skills articulated in the CCSS, while deepening student content knowledge.

Chapter 4: Meeting the Expectations of the Common Core. The CCSS is about college and career readiness. Classroom practices that foster independent learning and thinking are critical to developing college and career readiness skills. The tools in this chapter are designed to support your understanding and application of a focus and instructional practices that center on students.

Chapter 5: Addressing Text Complexity and Vocabulary. The CCSS establish the expectation that students need to read increasingly complex texts independently. As students engage in more complex texts, one of their greatest challenges is developing academic vocabulary. The tools in this chapter will develop your understanding of textual complexity and vocabulary in the CCSS.

Chapter 6: Differentiating the Standards. Although the CCSS do not advocate any particular instructional strategy, differentiating instruction is critical. Since the CCSS focuses on skill development, differentiated instruction supports the unique needs of individual learners as they develop skills.

Chapter 7: Schoolwide Common Core. Once you have explored the tools in the previous chapters to develop your understanding of the CCSS, it's time to look at implementation on a large schoolwide or district level. The tools in Chapter 7 support the development of this big picture.

Appendix. Tool #18: The CCSS ELA Grades 3–8 Matrices. For your convenience, I have included these printed graphic organizers for six core grade levels in English language arts. Feel free to fill in or duplicate these pages for use in PLCs and curriculum planning groups. *Important: These are only a sampling of available matrices.* A full set of standards matrices is included in the digital download for all grade levels and subject areas. See page ix for instructions on how to access the digital content.

Digital Content. The free downloadable content includes customizable versions of all reproducible forms in the book, along with over 300 pages of fill-in standards matrices for Tools #18–20. See page ix for instructions on how to access the digital content.

Finally, at the back of this book you will find a host of recommended resources on CCSS implementation. Aligning curriculum and instructional practice to the CCSS is a journey. The additional resources and information provide ongoing support in the Common Core era.

> All of the reproducible forms in this book are also available as digital files. See page ix for information on how and where to download them.

HOW TO USE THIS BOOK

Each educational context is unique. With this in mind, I designed this book to be a collection of resources that can meet the different needs of a variety of educational settings. If your school is just beginning to work with the CCSS, the first step is to examine the CCSS document. The tools in Chapter 1 of *The Common Sense Guide* will lead you through this process, so that you can develop a deep understanding of the standards and the skills that are articulated within. From there, the tools in successive chapters will support you and your colleagues through a curriculum audit as a foundation for Common Core integration and alignment. As you progress through the tools, you and your colleagues will prepare to embark on a plan for assessment, technology, and literacy integration on a schoolwide or districtwide level.

The sequential order of the tools provides a roadmap to understand and apply the CCSS. Feel free, however, to use the tools in whichever order fits your needs best. As you work through the tools, you might discover that some require more attention and in-depth discussion, while others are not needed for your purposes.

Keep in mind that completing all forty tools, or even half of them, as a busy educator, may appear overwhelming and burdensome. Try reviewing all of the tools before digging into any of them separately. Then, estimate how much time you have to devote and which of your needs are the most pressing. Once you've determined your time and priority needs, choose a handful of tools to start out with that feels doable. Do not feel pressured to complete each tool for every subject area, curriculum unit, and grade level you teach. You may find that you only need to use the tool for a couple of units or levels before you "get the hang of it" and are able to simplify the process going forward.

Following are examples of contexts in which you may work with these tools to foster collaboration with various stakeholders.

1. Professional development days. Over the past several years, I've used these tools at professional development workshops in more than twenty-five schools and districts to cultivate and support teachers' understanding of the CCSS.

2. Professional learning communities (PLCs). Two school districts, one in California and the other in Illinois, used each tool in this volume in separate forty- to fifty-minute professional learning community sessions. Through systematic study, teachers transition from learning about standards, to building curriculum, to planning for assessment.

3. Local professional development by administrators and district leaders. Administrators have used these tools with teachers, and district leaders have used them with administrators.

4. University teacher preparation programs. I present the tools in graduate-level teacher preparation classes. As my university students study to become educators, they must develop a thorough understanding of the CCSS and how these standards are compatible with research-based teaching methods.

5. Parents and community. The more parents and community leaders learn about the standards and their implications, the easier it will be to garner political and financial support to secure the resources needed to create twenty-first-century classrooms.

As I sit in front of my computer, you, my teacher colleagues, are on the forefront of my thoughts. I originally created these tools as part of my work in helping schools transition to the new standards. The actual CCSS document is packed with information, while *The Common Sense Guide to the Common Core* breaks down that information into smaller, usable chunks. My sole hope is that this resource will aid your work in the classroom.

Katherine S. McKnight, Ph.D.

Feel free to contact me through my website: www.katherinemcknight.com.

Chapter 1

Understanding the Common Core State Standards

Given the myths about the Common Core State Standards (CCSS) that were noted in the Introduction to this book, we need to go to the source to make sure that we have accurate information. The six tools in this chapter will guide you through the CCSS document so that you can identify the changes and what these mean for your classroom. The tools are designed to support your larger understanding of the standards, as well as delve into more specific elements of the CCSS, such as informational text and foundational skills in mathematics.

TOOLS #1–2: CLOSE READING AND EXAMINATION OF THE CCSS

The first two tools, on **pages 12 and 13,** are designed to walk you through a close reading of the standards. These tools are outlined with prompts that guide you through a step-by-step process toward understanding the meaning and impact of the new standards.

Note: The standards for literacy in the content areas (history/social studies, science, and technical subjects) are integrated into the English language arts (ELA) standards for kindergarten through fifth grade, and listed separately from the ELA standards for grades six through twelve. Tool #1 includes both ELA and literacy standards together, since they have a very similar structure and intent.

> **Important!** Before you begin, you'll need to acquire a copy of the CCSS document. Visit **www.corestandards.org/the-standards/download-the-standards** for free downloads of the entire document. Be sure to download *all* of the files: the introduction, applications, standards, and appendices. Plan to keep these PDF files handy for reference—on your computer desktop, tablet, or e-reader. Or, if you prefer, you can print them out.

Identify the four strands.	
What are clusters? *Hint:* See the beginning of the mathematics standards document for this answer.	
Give some examples of clusters.	
Locate a grade-level standard statement.	
Look at each strand. How many standards are included for each?	
For K–2: What are Reading Foundational Skills? Identify the grade levels at which these are addressed.	
Read Appendix A and identify key information that applies to you.	
Read Appendix B and identify key information that applies to you.	

Identify the four strands.	
What are clusters?	
Give some examples of clusters.	
Locate a grade-level standard statement.	
Look at each strand. How many standards are included for each?	
Read Appendix A and identify key information that applies to you.	
Read Appendix B and identify key information that applies to you.	

TOOLS #3–4: FOUNDATIONAL FEATURES OF THE CCSS

Unlike the first two tools, the following two "Foundational Features" tools are already filled in. They serve as reference tools that encapsulate the key features of the Common Core.

Tool #3: Foundational Features of the CCSS: ELA and Interdisciplinary Literacy, Grades K–12

As you read through the CCSS document, you can see many similarities between the ELA and content area literacy standards. Both sets of standards are aligned with the literacy anchor standards. Notice some important aspects: When reading the introduction to the Common Core State Standards, the development of literacy as a *shared responsibility* is noted in multiple instances. This means that literacy skills must be developed in all disciplines. You probably also noticed that narrative writing (CCSS.W.3) is included in the ELA standards but is omitted in the interdisciplinary literacy standards. This is a logical omission, because narrative writing is usually developed and included in the ELA content curriculum. Ultimately, the shared goal of both the ELA and content area literacy standards is to develop the same corpus of literacy skills within all aspects of a curriculum.

Tool #3, shown on **page 17,** summarizes the shifts in the following ELA and interdisciplinary literacy areas:

K–5 Balancing Informational and Literary Texts

The authors of the Common Core State Standards advocate for more informational texts (a type of nonfiction) to be included in the overall reading program because this is the kind of reading that students will most often encounter in college and careers:

> In accord with NAEP's growing emphasis on informational texts in the higher grades, the Standards demand that a significant amount of reading of informational texts take place in and outside the ELA classroom.[1]

Note, however, that although there is greater emphasis on informational text, this does not mean that literature should be forgotten or eliminated. In fact, the inclusion of both types of texts is called for to build a strong reading program (emphasis added):

> The Standards aim to align instruction with this framework so that many more students than at present can meet the requirements of college and career readiness. In grades K–5, the standards follow NAEP's lead in *balancing the reading of literature with the reading of informational texts,* including texts in history/social studies, science, and technical subjects.[2]

CCSS encourages educators to offer students a diet of both informational and literary texts in order to build essential reading skills.

---

[1] From *Common Core State Standards for English Language Arts & Literacy in History/Social Studies, Science, and Technical Subjects,* p. 5. National Governors Association Center for Best Practices and Council of Chief State School Officers.
[2] Ibid, p. 5.

6–12 Discipline Knowledge

You have probably heard the expression, "We are all teachers of reading and writing." Middle school and high school teachers possess strong content knowledge. Of course we need math teachers to be math teachers, and science teachers to be science teachers, and so on. However, all teachers need to be familiar with reading and writing pedagogies so that their students can develop greater comprehension of the content. We learn to read and then read to learn. Again, developing literacy skills is a *shared* responsibility that is not exclusive to English teachers. As explained in the CCSS document (emphasis added):

> *Reading is critical to building knowledge in history/social studies as well as in science and technical subjects.* College and career ready reading in these fields requires an appreciation of the norms and conventions of each discipline, such as the kinds of evidence used in history and science; an understanding of domain-specific words and phrases; an attention to precise details; and the capacity to evaluate intricate arguments, synthesize complex information, and follow detailed descriptions of events and concepts. *In history/social studies, for example, students need to be able to analyze, evaluate, and differentiate primary and secondary sources. When reading scientific and technical texts, students need to be able to gain knowledge from challenging texts that often make extensive use of elaborate diagrams and data to convey information and illustrate concepts. Students must be able to read complex informational texts in these fields* with independence and confidence because the *vast majority of reading in college and workforce training programs will be sophisticated nonfiction.* It is important to note that these Reading standards are meant to complement the specific content demands of the disciplines, not replace them.[1]

Complexity Staircase

Students are expected to be able to read increasingly challenging and complex texts as explained in the following (emphasis added):

> The Reading standards place equal emphasis on the sophistication of what students read and the skill with which they read. *Standard 10 defines a grade-by-grade "staircase" of increasing text complexity that rises from beginning reading to the college and career readiness level.*[2]

Given this expectation, educators are expected to provide students with a wide variety of texts that become increasingly challenging.

---

[1] Ibid., p. 60.
[2] Ibid., p. 8.

Text-Based Answers

Educators frequently express concern that personal response and connections to reading are not valued in CCSS. This is simply untrue as evidenced in the following section from the document (emphasis added):

> Whatever they are reading, *students must also show* a *steadily growing ability to discern more from and make fuller use of text*, including *making an increasing number of connections among ideas and between texts*, considering a wider range of textual evidence, and becoming more sensitive to inconsistencies, ambiguities, and poor reasoning in texts.[1]

What's different is that if a student makes a personal assertion or connection to a text it must now be supported with evidence from the text.

Drawing from Sources and Argument-Based Writing

The new standards emphasize the connection between reading and using text to support assertions, or claims in writing (emphasis added):

> The Standards acknowledge the fact that whereas some writing skills, such as the ability to plan, revise, edit, and publish, are applicable to many types of writing, other skills are more properly defined in terms of specific writing types: arguments, informative/explanatory texts, and narratives. Standard 9 stresses the *importance of the writing-reading connection by requiring students to draw upon and write about evidence from literary and informational texts.* Because of the centrality of writing to most forms of inquiry, research standards are prominently included in this strand, though skills important to research are infused throughout the document.[2]

The CCSS do not advocate a specific approach or formula for the teaching of writing. There are many different writing forms that can develop a claim and use textual evidence for support. Remember, as the CCSS introduction states: teachers are the best resource in determining the appropriate instructional methods for the development of student writing skills.

Academic Vocabulary

Through a close reading of the CCSS document, you probably noticed the verbs in the new standards. Students are expected to *analyze, apply, distinguish, assess, delineate,* and so on. Every student must possess proficiency in academic language in order to fully meet the CCSS expectations. Academic language is used in classrooms, in textbooks, and on tests. It is also used in some workplace environments. Academic language is different from conversational English.

---

[1] Ibid., p. 8.
[2] Ibid., p. 8.

Features	ELA Skills and Content Knowledge
K–5 Balancing Informational and Literary Texts	Students read a true balance of information and literary texts. At least 50 percent of what students read is informational.
6–12 Discipline Knowledge	Teachers outside of the ELA classroom emphasize literacy experiences and expand students' reading abilities to better learn the content.
Complexity Staircase	Each grade level requires a "step" of growth on the "staircase." Teachers support below-grade-level readers and create time and space in the curriculum for close and careful reading.
Text-Based Answers	Students develop habits for making evidentiary arguments, in both speaking and writing, in order to demonstrate comprehension of a text.
Drawing from Sources and Argument-Based Writing	Students develop the skills to formulate written, evidence-based arguments that respond to the ideas, facts, and arguments in the texts they read.
Academic Vocabulary	By focusing on pivotal and commonly found words, and less on esoteric literary terms, teachers build students' ability to access more complex texts across the content areas.

Tool #4: Foundational Features of the CCSS: Mathematics, Grades K–12

This tool, on **page 19,** summarizes the shifts in the following mathematics areas: focus, coherence, fluency, deep understanding, application, and dual intensity.

Consistent with the Common Core State Standards' emphasis on college and career readiness, teachers are expected to tackle three to four big ideas in mathematics at each grade level. This is a significant shift from many state standards, which were often long lists of topics and content material that a teacher would attempt to cover each year. The intention of the Common Core mathematics standards is to address fewer topics and explore them in greater depth. In this way, students develop greater skills and deeper understanding of more complex mathematics concepts (i.e., number sense). This is different from a week-to-week content focus that might look like a rapid succession of multiplication problems alternating with division problems. Instead, there are fewer topics that require students to apply newly acquired skills within rich contexts.

In addition, the CCSS offer greater coherence than past mathematical standards because the same large concepts are covered each year. This gives teachers the opportunity to develop these skills with increasingly complex content. Finally, the CCSS authors emphasize application and process. Students must be able to go beyond calculations and apply mathematics information to solve complex problems. They also must be able to use math effectively to access and interpret content in nonmath disciplines.

The Common Core State Standards for mathematics are quite detailed; some teachers may find them overwhelming. For additional insight, I suggest that you review the assessment examples in mathematics on the Smarter Balanced website and on the Partnership for Assessment of Readiness for College and Careers (PARCC) website. See page 134 for details.

Features	Mathematics Skills
Focus	Teachers focus deeply on the concepts that are prioritized in the standards. Students reach strong foundational knowledge and deep conceptual understanding. Students are able to transfer skills across concepts and grades.
Coherence	Principals and teachers carefully connect learning within and across grades so that concepts spiral across grade levels. Students build new understanding on foundations that were laid in previous years.
Fluency	Teachers structure class time and homework time for students to memorize core functions. Students are expected to have speed and accuracy with simple calculations.
Deep Understanding	Teachers not only teach how to get the answer, but also support each student's ability to access concepts from various perspectives. Students demonstrate understanding by applying core math concepts to new situations, as well as by writing and speaking about them.
Application	Teachers provide opportunities for students to apply math concepts in real-world situations; students are expected to choose the appropriate concept for application. Teachers in content areas outside of math ensure that students are using math to access and interpret content.
Dual Intensity	*Dual intensity* means that students will practice the skills they have, while gaining experience in choosing the opportunity in which to apply those skills. Teachers create opportunities for students to participate in drills and make use of those skills through extended application. The amount of time spent practicing skills and learning application varies, depending on the concept.

TOOL #5: UNDERSTANDING ACADEMIC LANGUAGE IN THE CCSS

The Common Core State Standards document is rich with academic language. Take a look at the group of standards in **Figure 1.1** and identify key academic terms that impact curriculum and instructional development. Tool #5 (**page 23 and Figure 1.2**) helps you identify these terms in the CCSS and develop a plan to put them into practice.

As you consider the reading standards for kindergarten through fifth grade shown in **Figure 1.1**, notice the academic language: *prompting, support, describe, identify, engage, compare, contrast, recognize, recount.* Now consider what these academic terms actually look like in practice. What do your students do that demonstrate using these terms?

FIGURE 1.1: READING STANDARDS FOR LITERATURE K–5

Reading Standards for Literature K–5

The following standards offer a focus for instruction each year and help ensure that students gain adequate exposure to a range of texts and tasks. Rigor is also infused through the requirement that students read increasingly complex texts through the grades. *Students advancing through the grades are expected to meet each year's grade-specific standards and retain or further develop skills and understandings mastered in preceding grades.*

Kindergartners:	Grade 1 Students:	Grade 2 Students:
Key Ideas and Details		
1. With prompting and support, ask and answer questions about key details in a text.	1. Ask and answer questions about key details in a text.	1. Ask and answer such questions as *who, what, where, when, why,* and *how* to demonstrate understanding of key details in a text.
2. With prompting and support, retell familiar stories, including key details.	2. Retell stories, including key details, and demonstrate understanding of their central message or lesson.	2. Recount stories, including fables and folktales from diverse cultures, and determine their central message, lesson, or moral.
3. With prompting and support, identify characters, settings, and major events in a story.	3. Describe characters, settings, and major events in a story, using key details.	3. Describe how characters in a story respond to major events and challenges.
Craft and Structure		
4. Ask and answer questions about unknown words in a text.	4. Identify words and phrases in stories or poems that suggest feelings or appeal to the senses.	4. Describe how words and phrases (e.g., regular beats, alliteration, rhymes, repeated lines) supply rhythm and meaning in a story, poem, or song.
5. Recognize common types of texts (e.g., storybooks, poems).	5. Explain major differences between books that tell stories and books that give information, drawing on a wide reading of a range of text types.	5. Describe the overall structure of a story, including describing how the beginning introduces the story and the ending concludes the action.
6. With prompting and support, name the author and illustrator of a story and define the role of each in telling the story.	6. Identify who is telling the story at various points in a text.	6. Acknowledge differences in the points of view of characters, including by speaking in a different voice for each character when reading dialogue aloud.
Integration of Knowledge and Ideas		
7. With prompting and support, describe the relationship between illustrations and the story in which they appear (e.g., what moment in a story an illustration depicts).	7. Use illustrations and details in a story to describe its characters, setting, or events.	7. Use information gained from the illustrations and words in a print or digital text to demonstrate understanding of its characters, setting, or plot.
8. (Not applicable to literature)	8. (Not applicable to literature)	8. (Not applicable to literature)
9. With prompting and support, compare and contrast the adventures and experiences of characters in familiar stories.	9. Compare and contrast the adventures and experiences of characters in stories.	9. Compare and contrast two or more versions of the same story (e.g., Cinderella stories) by different authors or from different cultures.
Range of Reading and Level of Text Complexity		
10. Actively engage in group reading activities with purpose and understanding.	10. With prompting and support, read prose and poetry of appropriate complexity for grade 1.	10. By the end of the year, read and comprehend literature, including stories and poetry, in the grades 2–3 text complexity band proficiently, with scaffolding as needed at the high end of the range.

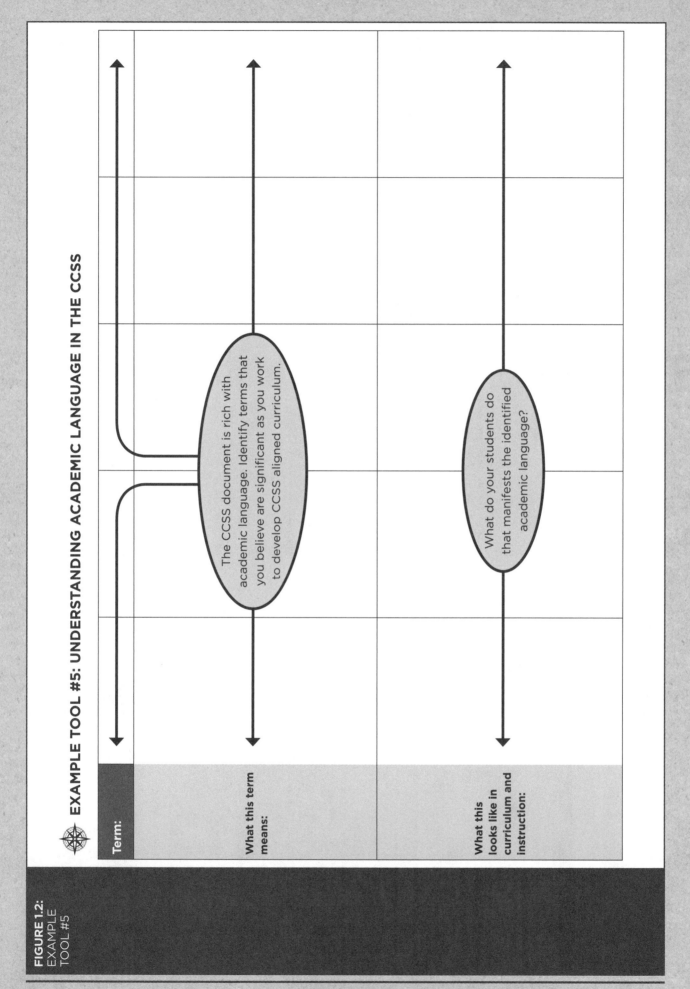

FIGURE 1.2:
EXAMPLE
TOOL #5

EXAMPLE TOOL #5: UNDERSTANDING ACADEMIC LANGUAGE IN THE CCSS

Term:

What this term means:

The CCSS document is rich with academic language. Identify terms that you believe are significant as you work to develop CCSS aligned curriculum.

What this looks like in curriculum and instruction:

What do your students do that manifests the identified academic language?

Term:		
What this term means:		
What this looks like in curriculum and instruction:		

TOOL #6: FULCRUM AND FOCUS STANDARDS

The CCSS are substantial, and it takes time and expertise to determine what they mean for different school contexts. In my work in developing CCSS-aligned curricula with educators, we use Tool #6 to identify which standards are large goals, or focus standards, and which ones may take years to develop—fulcrum standards (**page 26 and Figure 1.3**). For example, Reading Anchor Standard 10, "Read and comprehend complex literary and informational texts independently and proficiently"[1] is an example of what I call a *fulcrum standard*. This kind of standard is a long-term goal that is not easily articulated and achieved at a lesson or unit level. The anchor standards for reading and for mathematics are generally fulcrum standards.

Focus standards, on the other hand, are the ones that can be addressed on a lesson or unit level. The focus standards are the grade-level articulations of the anchor standards. Here's an example:

With prompting and support, ask and answer questions about key details in a text.[2]

We could break down the grade-level articulation in focus standards even further and create "I Can" statements, or lesson-level objectives. Here's an example:

Focus Standard:

With prompting and support, ask and answer questions about key details in a text.

"I Can" Statements:

- I can answer questions about the text with help from my teacher or a friend.

- I can answer questions and give examples from the text that explain my answer with some help or on my own.

- I can ask questions about the text.

See page 58 for more about developing "I Can" Statements.

---

[1] CCSS.ELA-Literacy.CCRA.R.1
[2] CCSS.ELA-Literacy.R.K.1

EXAMPLE TOOL #6: FULCRUM AND FOCUS STANDARDS

Standard	Fulcrum	Focus	How does this standard fit into your curriculum? List "I Can" statements.
With prompting and support, ask and answer questions about key details in a text. (CCSS.ELA-Literacy.R.K.1)		✓	• *I can answer questions about the text with help from my teacher or a friend.* • *I can answer questions and give examples from the text that explain my answer with some help or on my own.* • *I can ask questions about the text.*

Each grade-level standard should be identified as either a fulcrum or focus standard.

Goal-oriented standards, often anchor standards

Usually occur at the unit or lesson level, often grade-level standards

Explain how the identified standard will fit into the curriculum and instruction, using "I Can" statements.

Standard	Fulcrum	Focus	How does this standard fit into your curriculum? List "I Can" statements.

Chapter 2
Analyzing Your Current Standards and Curriculum

Now that you have examined the Common Core document, it's time to revisit your existing standards and curriculum, for the sake of comparing and contrasting. The six tools in this chapter are designed to help you audit your current curriculum and practice against the expectations of the Common Core State Standards (CCSS). Examining your current practices will make it easier to plan how to meet the standards. I am certain that you are already providing instruction that reflects many of the expectations of the CCSS, yet an audit is necessary to identify where you need to revise curriculum and instruction to meet all of the expectations of the CCSS.

TOOL #7: IDENTIFYING PARADIGM SHIFTS IN THE CCSS

As you explore the CCSS, consider where you have been with previous standards. The first generation, which were state based, have some overlap with the new Common Core State Standards. Many teachers panic that they will have to start all over again with this new initiative. This is not the case.

The first step in transitioning is to examine the current standards that your school or district uses to develop curriculum and instruction. These standards could be state-based standards, the college readiness standards, or other groups of standards that articulate the expectations of what students will know and be able to do. As you go through your current standards, highlight those areas that don't align with the CCSS.

Once you have finished examining your current standards, fill out Tool #7 (**page 30 and Figure 2.1**). In the first column, under the heading *Content Area*, identify the changes in the teaching of specific content. For example, the new Common Core State Standards emphasize argumentation in writing more strongly than most current state-based standards. If that's true for your school, you may want to list "argumentation in writing" in this column. In the adjacent column labeled *Change in Content*, important information about this paradigm shift should be listed. So, as I look closely at Writing Standard 1 (describing the expectations for argumentation in writing), I might choose to list that the new standards use the term *claim* instead of *thesis*, or *main idea*.

Here's another example, this time from mathematics. Currently, in many school districts, money is taught in first and second grades. The new standards focus on related concepts like "understanding place value" in first grade and shift the specific focus on money to second grade. If you're a first or second grade teacher and this represents a curriculum change in your school district, you may want to list "money" in the *Content Area* column, and write something like "place value first grade, money second grade" in the adjacent *Change* column.

In planning for the new standards, examining current practices and paradigms helps you identify how to best meet the fidelity of the new standards. This tool helps you focus on changes to relevant curricula in specific classrooms, which will help you avoid feeling overwhelmed by the entire body of standards as you prepare students for college and careers.

FIGURE 2.1:
EXAMPLE
TOOL #7

✦ **EXAMPLE TOOL #7: IDENTIFYING PARADIGM SHIFTS IN THE CCSS**

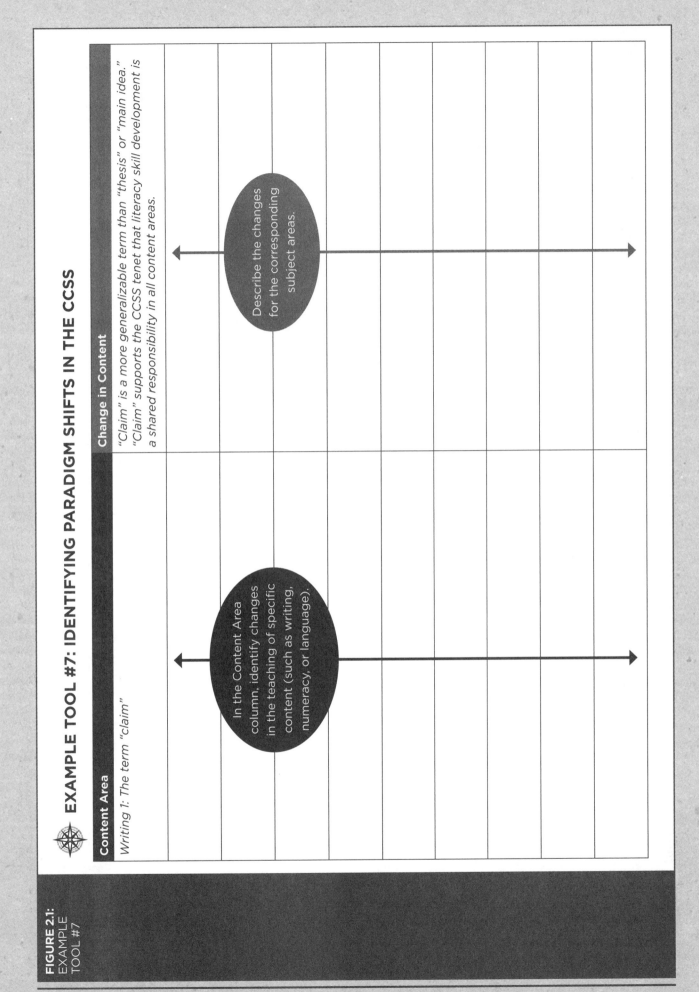

Content Area	Change in Content
Writing 1: The term "claim"	*"Claim" is a more generalizable term than "thesis" or "main idea." "Claim" supports the CCSS tenet that literacy skill development is a shared responsibility in all content areas.*

In the Content Area column, identify changes in the teaching of specific content (such as writing, numeracy, or language).

Describe the changes for the corresponding subject areas.

IDENTIFYING PARADIGM SHIFTS IN THE CCSS

Content Area	Change in Content

TOOL #8: COMPARING THE STANDARDS

Once you have been able to identify the paradigm shifts in the CCSS, Tool #8 will allow you to dig more deeply into the standards. Think of the big shifts as being on the macro level, while the actual standards are on the micro level of the new Common Core expectations.

Tool #8 (**page 33 and Figure 2.2**) is designed to analyze the current standards that your school or district uses and compare them to the Common Core State Standards. This tool helps you evaluate the current expectations for teaching and learning in state standards and then identify how the standards are markedly different from or similar to the CCSS.

To use this tool, list your current state standard in the first column. Next, identify a corresponding CCSS in the second column. The third column prompts you to examine how the current standard and the CCSS you listed are similar. Then, in the fourth column, you note how they're different. Finally, after you've filled in the first four columns comparing your current state standard to the new one, use the far right column to state how this information will assist you in aligning curriculum and instruction to the Common Core State Standards.

✦ **EXAMPLE TOOL #8: COMPARING THE STANDARDS**

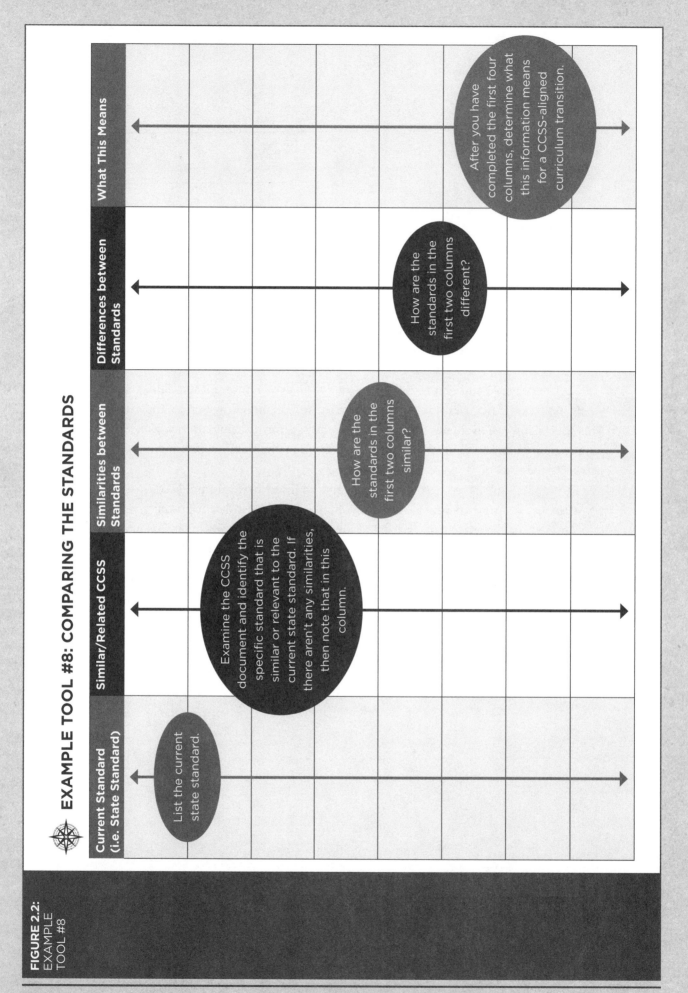

Current Standard (i.e. State Standard)	Similar/Related CCSS	Similarities between Standards	Differences between Standards	What This Means

List the current state standard.

Examine the CCSS document and identify the specific standard that is similar or relevant to the current state standard. If there aren't any similarities, then note that in this column.

How are the standards in the first two columns similar?

How are the standards in the first two columns different?

After you have completed the first four columns, determine what this information means for a CCSS-aligned curriculum transition.

COMPARING THE STANDARDS

Current Standard (i.e. State Standard)	Similar/Related CCSS	Similarities between Standards	Differences between Standards	What This Means

TOOL #9: GAP ANALYSIS

As I mentioned previously, many teachers across the country are concerned that the new standards will require them to completely rewrite current curriculum. If you are engaging in strong, research-based teaching and learning methodologies, this fear will most likely be unfounded for you. To confirm this, however, you must conduct a close analysis of the current curriculum and instructional practice in your school and compare it to the expectations of the Common Core State Standards.

While Tool #8, Comparing the Standards, focuses on a macro level, Tool #9 (**page 36 and Figure 2.3**) drills down to the micro level and assists teachers with a detailed comparison of their current practices with the new standards. Once teachers have completed this analysis, they can more easily identify the gaps between the previous state-based standards and the CCSS. When these gaps are identified, teachers and curriculum specialists can address the discrepancies and develop a plan to address them. Plans might include new instructional approaches such as mastery learning, project-based learning, or backward design as a means to create curriculum that better meets the expectations of the Common Core.

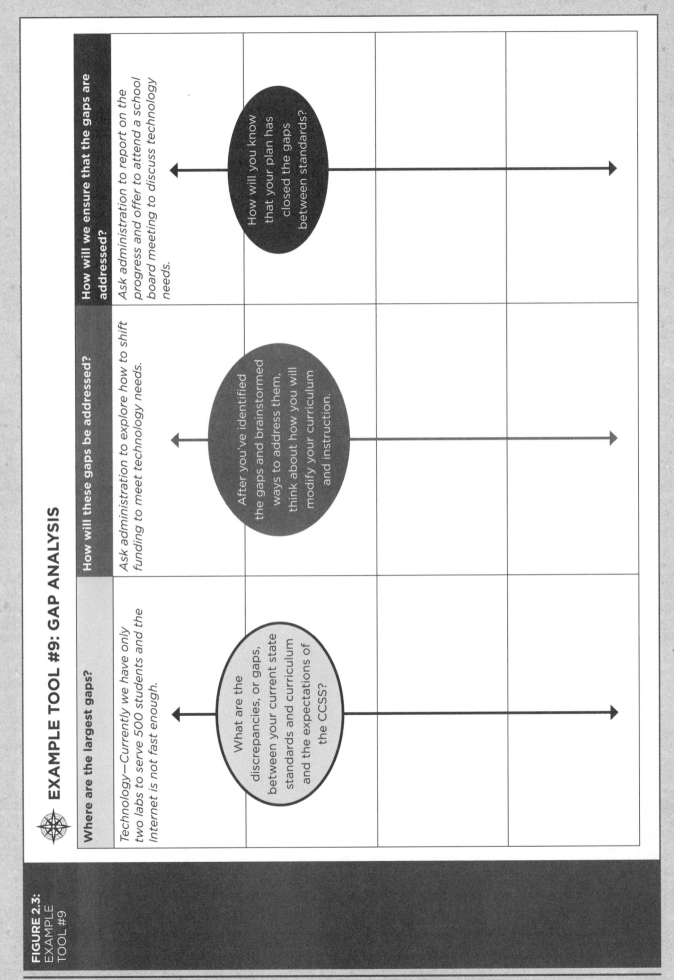

EXAMPLE TOOL #9: GAP ANALYSIS

Where are the largest gaps?	How will these gaps be addressed?	How will we ensure that the gaps are addressed?
Technology—Currently we have only two labs to serve 500 students and the Internet is not fast enough.	Ask administration to explore how to shift funding to meet technology needs.	Ask administration to report on the progress and offer to attend a school board meeting to discuss technology needs.

What are the discrepancies, or gaps, between your current state standards and curriculum and the expectations of the CCSS?

After you've identified the gaps and brainstormed ways to address them, think about how you will modify your curriculum and instruction.

How will you know that your plan has closed the gaps between standards?

Where are the largest gaps?	How will these gaps be addressed?	How will we ensure that the gaps are addressed?

TOOL #10: CURRICULUM AUDIT

Now that you have identified the gaps that block your ability to meet the standards, the purpose of Tool #10 (**page 39 and Figure 2.4**) is to assist you in determining long-term curriculum and instructional goals, based on the CCSS. In the first circle, identify what is already powerful and strong in your curriculum. In the second circle, identify the curriculum goals that you have for students in your particular school context. For example, it might be more technology integration or more emphasis in writing in the content areas. In the third circle, identify existing components in your curriculum that can contribute to a stronger curriculum that meets the expectations of the Common Core State Standards. In the fourth circle, list the resources your school needs in order to create your ideal CCSS-compliant curriculum.

EXAMPLE TOOL #10: CURRICULUM AUDIT

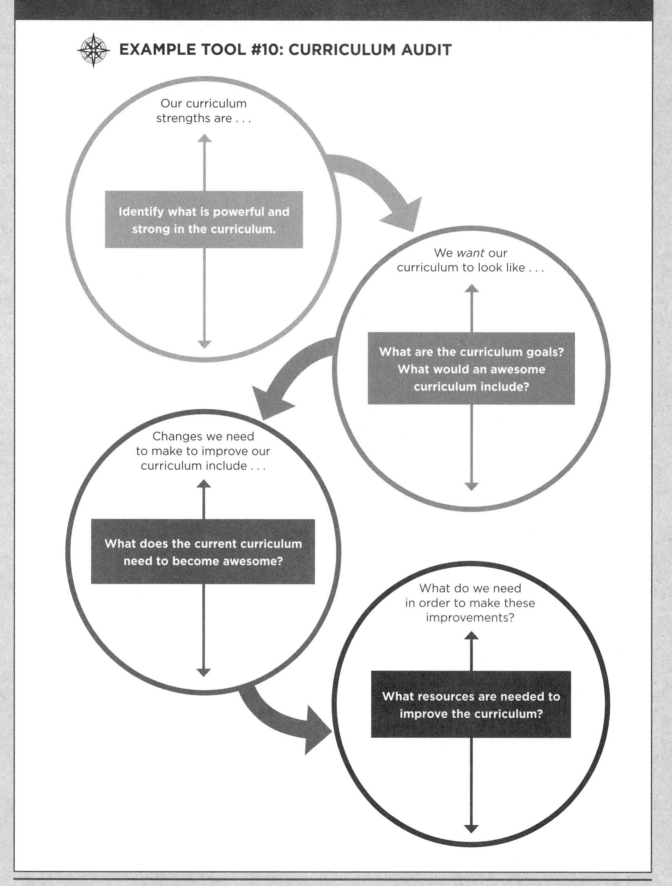

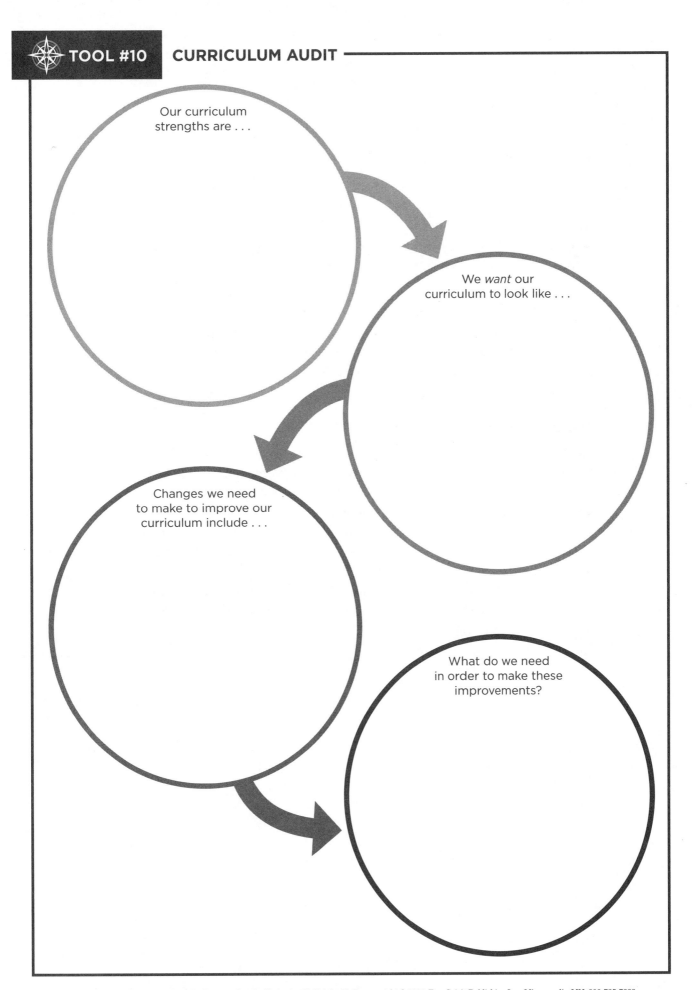

Our curriculum strengths are . . .

We *want* our curriculum to look like . . .

Changes we need to make to improve our curriculum include . . .

What do we need in order to make these improvements?

TOOLS #11–12: CURRICULUM STRENGTHS AND WEAKNESSES

Curriculum and instructional changes must be informed by data that includes standardized or more formalized assessments, as well as by teacher input and classroom-based data. As you implement the CCSS, using data and teacher input is essential in determining the current strengths and weaknesses of your school curriculum. Once the strengths and weaknesses are identified, your school community can create a plan for successful implementation.

Tool #11: Curriculum Strengths

I have no doubt that you and your colleagues are already teaching a curriculum that is largely Common Core–ready. Tool #11 (**page 42 and Figure 2.5**) is designed to identify the strengths of your current curriculum and use data sources to support these assertions. In the first column, labeled *Curriculum Strength*, identify and list what you believe are the strengths of your current curriculum. In the second column, provide the data that identifies each strength. State assessment data, school-based data, student grades, and teacher-created assessments can all assist in identifying your curriculum strengths. In the third column, enter other evidence that this area is a strength. This includes information that may not be represented through quantitative assessments. For example, student motivation and engagement are not easily measured but are crucial in assessing the positive impact of identified curriculum content.

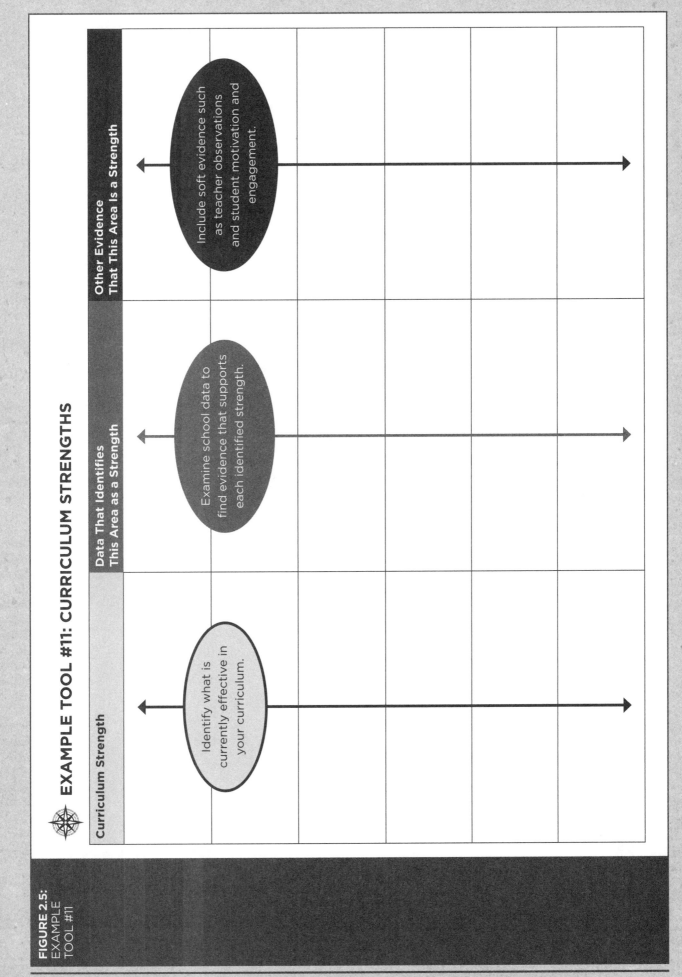

FIGURE 2.5:
EXAMPLE
TOOL #11

EXAMPLE TOOL #11: CURRICULUM STRENGTHS

Curriculum Strength	Data That Identifies This Area as a Strength	Other Evidence That This Area Is a Strength
Identify what is currently effective in your curriculum.	Examine school data to find evidence that supports each identified strength.	Include soft evidence such as teacher observations and student motivation and engagement.

CURRICULUM STRENGTHS

Curriculum Strength	Data That Identifies This Area as a Strength	Other Evidence That This Area Is a Strength

Tool #12: Curriculum Weaknesses

In contrast to Tool #11, Tool #12 (**page 45 and Figure 2.6**) is designed to help you identify what needs to be revised and restructured in your current curriculum as you implement the Common Core State Standards. After a close reading of the new standards, identify the weaknesses of your current curriculum and use data sources to support these assertions. In the first column, *Curriculum Weakness*, identify and list what you believe are the weaknesses in the current curriculum. In the second column, provide the data that identifies each area of weakness. State assessment data, school-based data, student grades, and teacher-created assessments can all assist in identifying your curriculum weaknesses. In the third column, enter other evidence that this area is a weakness. This includes information that may not be represented through quantitative assessments. *Note:* The tools in Chapter 3 will help you shore up these weaknesses.

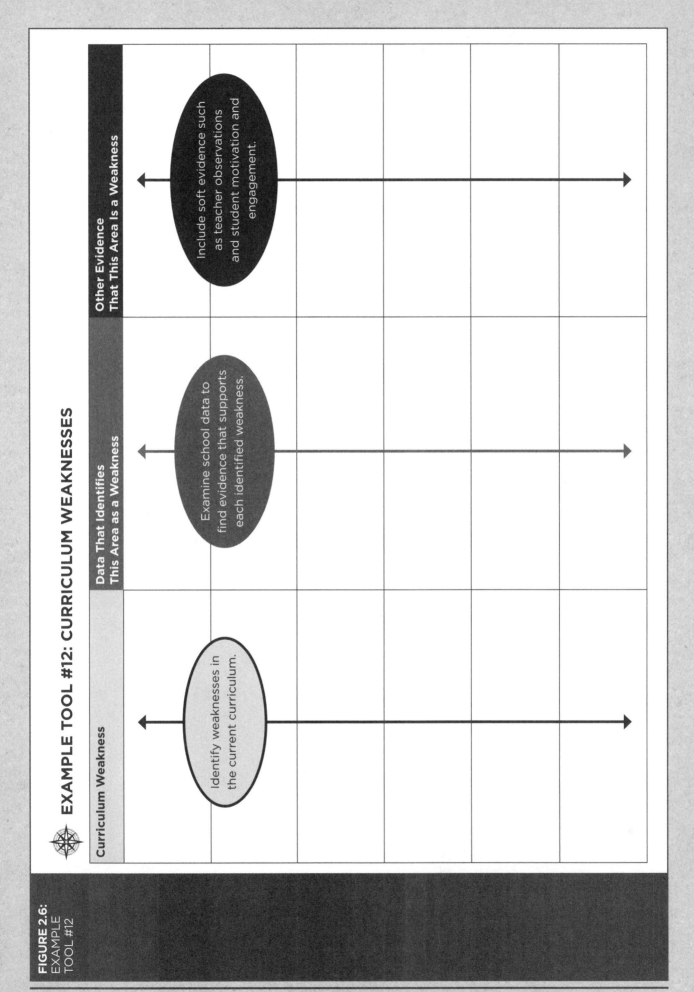

FIGURE 2.6:
EXAMPLE
TOOL #12

EXAMPLE TOOL #12: CURRICULUM WEAKNESSES

Curriculum Weakness	Data That Identifies This Area as a Weakness	Other Evidence That This Area Is a Weakness
Identify weaknesses in the current curriculum.	Examine school data to find evidence that supports each identified weakness.	Include soft evidence such as teacher observations and student motivation and engagement.

CURRICULUM WEAKNESSES

Curriculum Weakness	Data That Identifies This Area as a Weakness	Other Evidence That This Area Is a Weakness

Chapter 3
Transitioning to the Common Core

In Chapters 1 and 2, you closely examined the standards and then compared them to the current curriculum and instruction in your context. Now you are ready to develop a transition plan. The eight tools in this chapter will help you and your colleagues assemble a schoolwide or districtwide plan to transition to the Common Core State Standards (CCSS) on a larger scale.

TOOL #13: SCHOOLWIDE TRANSITION PLAN

Creating a coherent plan is essential for an entire school to successfully transition to the Common Core State Standards. Administrators and faculty need to work as a team to identify how to revise curriculum and adopt pedagogical practices. This is a big project that cannot be completed instantaneously; instead, it's a process. Working together to reach agreement on your priorities leads to the best outcomes. Tool #13 (**page 48**) outlines the process that schools can use for transitioning to the Common Core.

In step one of this tool, *Perform close study of standards*, summarize how you and your colleagues will identify the most critical features for your school. In step two, *Identify current instructional standards that support the CCSS*, examine what instructional practices are in place that are already meeting the expectations of the new standards. Don't throw out your curriculum! Instead, use it as a foundation to examine and reflect on your instructional practice. Document this information in step three, *Identify areas of the curriculum to align with the CCSS*. Once the first three steps are completed, you're ready for step four, in which you *Document areas of the curriculum that don't align with the CCSS*.

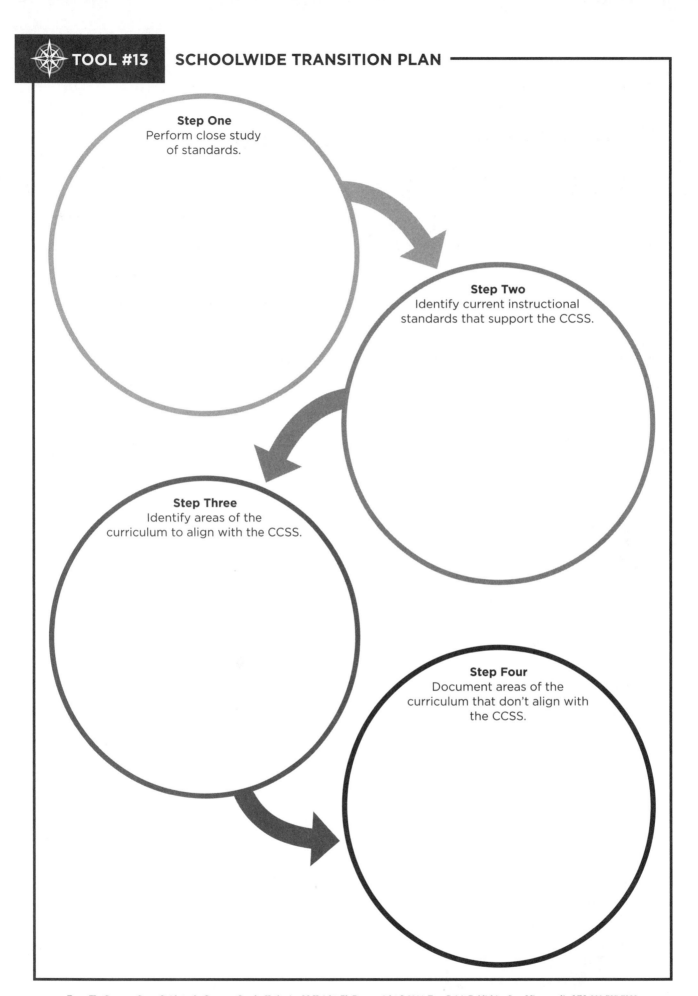

Step One
Perform close study
of standards.

Step Two
Identify current instructional
standards that support the CCSS.

Step Three
Identify areas of the
curriculum to align with the CCSS.

Step Four
Document areas of the
curriculum that don't align with
the CCSS.

TOOL #14: IDENTIFYING NEEDS WHILE TRANSITIONING

Because the Common Core State Standards represent a tremendous paradigm shift to prepare students for twenty-first-century careers, the ways in which we think about classroom materials and structures must evolve. The authors of the CCSS recognize this shift, which is demonstrated through the skills focus and the technology integration.

Upon completing a close reading and analysis of the new standards, you might realize that you need new resources. For example, Reading Anchor Standard 10 states that students should be able to "read and comprehend complex literary and informational texts independently and proficiently." This means that students should be able to read a wide variety of texts. Limiting reading to the textbook does not provide the opportunity for students to encounter many different texts. Remember, the CCSS does not advocate one particular strategy or methodology, so omitting textbooks is not a suggestion found in the document. Yet, according to reading research, students who read a lot of grade-level materials will increase their ability to meet the expectations for standard 10.[1]

Now let's look at how Tool #14 (**page 51 and Figure 3.1**) can help you identify and address resource needs. Continuing the example with Reading Anchor Standard 10, under the *Need* column on the left side of this tool, you might list, "Sample reading materials in all subject areas, in addition to or in place of a textbook." The right-hand column is essentially an action plan. While brainstorming with colleagues, you can use this column to record the ways in which funding for materials could be allocated to ensure that student reading materials are widely available.

---

[1] Heller & Greenleaf, 2007; International Reading Association, 2000; Carver, 2000; Chall, 2000.

EXAMPLE TOOL #14: IDENTIFYING NEEDS WHILE TRANSITIONING

Need	How will this need be addressed?
More trade books are needed to differentiate texts for reading levels in order to meet Reading Anchor Standard 10	Analyze reading textbooks for reading levels and evaluate whether these materials are meeting the varied reading needs of the students. Allot funding to purchase more trade books.

What resources (e.g., computers, books, professional development) are needed?

How can each resource need be addressed (e.g., more funding or reallocation of resources)?

IDENTIFYING NEEDS WHILE TRANSITIONING

How will this need be addressed?	Need

TOOLS #15–16: MAPPING CURRICULUM

Since the Common Core State Standards promote a focus on the application and demonstration of skills, curriculums must reflect this change. This means you need to look at curriculum mapping a bit differently. Most schools and districts are wisely using the Understanding by Design (UBD) model for planning instruction.[1] With this model you begin by creating the assessment that will measure students' mastery of a particular standard. Your assessment design takes into account the required content knowledge and performance indicators that demonstrate students have developed the required skill. Then you plan the instruction around a really great essential question or questions.

In the UBD model, an essential question is one that promotes the *how* and the *why*. Some examples of essential questions might include, *How do shapes help us understand our world?* or *What drives a population to revolt?* These are the kinds of questions that encourage students to explore and learn new content information while developing skills. (See Tool #23 on page 73 for more on writing essential questions.)

Tools #15 and #16 (**pages 53 and 54**) help facilitate curriculum mapping in units for English language arts (ELA) and interdisciplinary literacy and for math.

---

[1] Wiggins and McTighe, 2005

MAPPING CURRICULUM: ELA AND INTERDISCIPLINARY LITERACY UNIT DESIGN

UNIT/CHAPTER DESIGN

Essential Question(s):

Unit/Chapter Title:		Unit Length:
Course/Grade:		Date Created:

Unit Vocabulary/Concepts/Topics

Define and use unit vocabulary.

1.

2.

3.

4.

5.

6.

Assessment or Evidence of Learning:

MAPPING CURRICULUM: MATH UNIT DESIGN

UNIT/CHAPTER DESIGN

Essential Question(s):

Unit/Chapter Title:		Unit Length:
Course/Grade:		Date Created:

Unit Vocabulary/Concepts/Topics

Define and use unit vocabulary.

1.

2.

3.

4.

5.

6.

Mathematics Skills Featured in This Unit:

Assessment or Evidence of Learning:

TOOL #17: COMPATIBLE CURRICULUM DESIGN FOR THE CCSS

In the summer of 2011, I worked with more than thirty educators to develop K–12 ELA CCSS-aligned curriculum maps. We engaged in many discussions about how to best achieve fidelity. Eventually we concluded that a curriculum model that was designed around an essential question and that required knowledge tasks and performance tasks would be the best design to meet the rigorous CCSS. Building on the Understanding by Design model and the Universal Design for Learning principles, we created the curriculum maps. Since then I have worked with other schools and districts to create CCSS-aligned curriculum maps for both mathematics and English language arts, using Tools #15 and #16. Each time, the teachers decided that integrating essential questions along with knowledge and performance tasks would be the most effective curriculum model for the new standards. Tool #17 (**page 57 and Figure 3.2**) is the most recent version of my design template for curriculum mapping.

EXAMPLE TOOL #17: COMPATIBLE CURRICULUM DESIGN FOR THE CCSS

Unit Name/Length of Unit: *Ethnic Cultures/3 weeks*

Description of Unit: *Fifth grade students will learn about different ethnic cultures and explore and identify characteristics of a culture. The students will also examine how different cultures impacted the development and identity of the United States.*

Essential Question(s): *What can other cultures teach us about ourselves?*

Common Core Focus Standards Addressed:

RF.5.4: *Read with sufficient accuracy and fluency to support comprehension.*

RF.5.4(c): *Use context to confirm or self-correct word recognition and understanding, rereading as necessary.*

W.5.1: *Write opinion pieces on topics or texts, supporting a point of view with reasons and information.*

SL.5.3: *Summarize the points a speaker makes and explain how each claim is supported by reasons and evidence.*

L.5.1: *Demonstrate command of the conventions of standard English grammar and usage when writing or speaking.*

L.5.4(c): *Consult reference materials (e.g., dictionaries, glossaries, thesauruses), both print and digital, to find the pronunciation and determine or clarify the precise meaning of key words and phrases.*

KNOWLEDGE TASKS

The students will study a variety of primary source documents about immigration and ethnic cultures. The students will also read a wide variety of texts that will develop their content knowledge about culture and different cultures that immigrated to the United States.
In groups, the students will select a culture to study in depth.
The students will engage in discussions regarding related texts, music, art, and primary source documents on various cultures.

PERFORMANCE TASKS

The students will:
Create an argumentation-based piece of writing that focuses on how a specific culture positively impacted the United States.
Design an informative Google site about the selected culture that includes information about tribal organization, laws, culture, and traditions.

Literacy Integration and Corresponding CCSS (for grades 6–12 only):
Not applicable

Academic Vocabulary:
Students will learn social studies content vocabulary including:
culture, dominant culture, tradition, immigration, ethnic, migration

Unit Name/Length of Unit:

Description of Unit:

Essential Question(s):

Common Core Focus Standards Addressed:

KNOWLEDGE TASKS

PERFORMANCE TASKS

Literacy Integration and Corresponding CCSS (for grades 6–12 only):

Academic Vocabulary:

TOOLS #18–20: SAMPLE STANDARDS MATRICES

As you plan to transition to the CCSS, you and your colleagues will need to map out standards for an entire grade level. The tools on **pages 59, 60, and 62** will help you with that process. But first, let's review how the Common Core defines the following terms:

1. Anchor standards. At the top of the standards hierarchy, the anchor standards are sometimes misunderstood as actual lessons or as unit-level standards, objectives, or learning targets. This is not the case. Think of the anchor standards as a high-level cloud that encompasses the entire K–12 student experience. The anchor standards provide a way of thinking, or a way of being, as students develop the skills that they need to achieve college and career readiness by the end of twelfth grade. Lessons and units do not contain whole anchor standards. The anchor standards may be referred to in lesson or unit planning, but it would be impossible to align a lesson or unit to one of them.

2. Grade-level standards. The next level in the Common Core structure is grade-level standards. These grade-level articulations are designed to convey the expectations for students at the end of that corresponding grade level.

3. Unit-level and lesson-level standards. Depending on your school or district, you may refer to the statements that comprise this lowest level of standards as learning objectives, learning targets, or focus statements. In this book, they are referred to as "*I Can*" *statements*, because they come from the student's perspective (see page 24 for more details). Teaching is about the students, always. When you write statements for a unit- and lesson-level curriculum that are from a student perspective, you facilitate educators' understanding of how to support students in developing the CCSS-articulated skills.

The matrices in Tools #18–20 are designed to help you examine the anchor and grade-level standards first. In the second column, *Converted/Unpacked Standard,* you draft unit-level and lesson-level "I Can" statements that support the larger framework. In the third column, *Observations from Analysis,* record your thoughts about what the unpacked standards mean for your students, using test data, classroom experiences, and your teacher expertise. Remember, no one knows your students better than you do. Some examples might be: *Need more modeling to write effective questions* or *The students are great at who/what/where questions but need to learn how to develop more critical how and why questions.* In the final column, focus on learning progressions and scaffolding. Keep in mind that the first column, the CCSS grade-level articulation, is a year-end goal. Maybe in the first ten weeks of school you develop the students' skills in asking simpler questions, and then you gradually build up to more complex questions by week twenty.

> **Important!** The Appendix on pages 135–225 contains the Tool #18 standards matrices for ELA, grades 3–8. Additionally, the digital content includes customizable matrices for all grade levels and subjects areas. See page ix for instructions on how to access the digital content.

Unpack the CCSS and articulate each standard from a student point of view. Use school data and teacher observation to add details and information regarding each standard.

CCSS	Converted/Unpacked Standard	Observations from Analysis	When in the year will this standard be covered?
Reading Standards for Literature			
CC.2.R.L.1 Key Ideas and Details: Ask and answer such questions as who, what, where, when, why, and how to demonstrate understanding of key details in a text.	**Example:** *I can answer who, what, where, when, and why questions to show that I understand the text.*		
CC.2.R.L.2 Key Ideas and Details: Recount stories, including fables and folktales from diverse cultures, and determine their central message, lesson, or moral.			
CC.2.R.L.3 Key Ideas and Details: Describe how characters in a story respond to major events and challenges.			
CC.2.R.L.4 Craft and Structure: Describe how words and phrases (e.g., regular beats, alliteration, rhymes, repeated lines) supply rhythm and meaning in a story, poem, or song.			
CC.2.R.L.5 Craft and Structure: Describe the overall structure of a story, including describing how the beginning introduces the story and the ending concludes the action.			
CC.2.R.L.6 Craft and Structure: Acknowledge differences in the points of view of characters, including by speaking in a different voice for each character when reading dialogue aloud.			

From *Common Core State Standards for English Language Arts & Literacy in History/Social Studies, Science, and Technical Subjects.*
Copyright © 2010. National Governors Association Center for Best Practices and Council of Chief State School Officers. All rights reserved.

*NOTE: This is just one sample excerpt; the full collection of all ELA standards at all grade levels is included in the digital download. See page ix for instructions on how to access.

Unpack the CCSS and articulate each standard from a student point of view.
Use school data and teacher observation to add details and information regarding each standard.

CCSS	Converted/Unpacked Standard	Observations from Analysis	When in the year will this standard be covered?
Reading Standards for Literacy in History/Social Studies 6-12			
CC.ELA-Literacy.RH.9-10.1 Key Ideas and Details: Cite specific textual evidence to support analysis of primary and secondary sources, attending to such features as the date and origin of the information.	**Examples:** *I can identify evidence from the text to support my analysis.* *I can cite primary and secondary sources to support my analysis.* *I can evaluate the information to determine if it will support my analysis.*		
CC.ELA-Literacy.RH.9-10.2 Key Ideas and Details: Determine the central ideas or information of a primary or secondary source; provide an accurate summary of how key events or ideas develop over the course of the text.			
CC.ELA-Literacy.RH.9-10.3 Key Ideas and Details: Analyze in detail a series of events described in a text; determine whether earlier events caused later ones or simply preceded them.			
CC.ELA-Literacy.RH.9-10.4 Craft and Structure: Determine the meaning of words and phrases as they are used in a text, including vocabulary describing political, social, or economic aspects of history/social science.			
CC.ELA-Literacy.RH.9-10.5 Craft and Structure: Analyze how a text uses structure to emphasize key points or advance an explanation or analysis.			

CONTINUED ON NEXT PAGE

*NOTE: This is just one sample excerpt; the full collection of all ELA standards at all grade levels is included in the digital download. See page ix for instructions on how to access.

From *Common Core State Standards for English Language Arts & Literacy in History/Social Studies, Science, and Technical Subjects.*
Copyright © 2010. National Governors Association Center for Best Practices and Council of Chief State School Officers. All rights reserved.

CCSS	Converted/Unpacked Standard	Observations from Analysis	When in the year will this standard be covered?
Reading Standards for Literacy in History/Social Studies 6–12			
CC.ELA-Literacy.RH.9-10.6 Craft and Structure: Compare the point of view of two or more authors for how they treat the same or similar topics, including which details they include and emphasize in their respective accounts.			
CC.ELA-Literacy.RH.9-10.7 Integration of Knowledge and Ideas: Integrate quantitative or technical analysis (e.g., charts, research data) with qualitative analysis in print or digital text.			
CC.ELA-Literacy.RH.9-10.8 Integration of Knowledge and Ideas: Assess the extent to which the reasoning and evidence in a text support the author's claims.			
CC.ELA-Literacy.RH.9-10.9 Integration of Knowledge and Ideas: Compare and contrast treatments of the same topic in several primary and secondary sources.			
CC.ELA-Literacy.RH.9-10.10 Range of Reading and Level of Text Complexity: By the end of grade 10, read and comprehend history/social studies texts in the grades 9–10 text complexity band independently and proficiently.			

Unpack the CCSS and articulate each standard from a student point of view.
Use school data and teacher observation to add details and information regarding each standard.

CCSS	Converted/Unpacked Standard	Observations from Analysis	When in the year will this standard be covered?
The Number System			
CC.8.NS.1. Know that numbers that are not rational are called irrational. Understand informally that every number has a decimal expansion; the rational numbers are those with decimal expansions that terminate in zeroes or eventually repeat. Know that other numbers are called irrational.	**Example:** *I can show that every number has a decimal expansion.*		
CC.8.NS.2 Use rational approximations of irrational numbers to compare the size of irrational numbers, locate them approximately on a number line diagram, and estimate the value of expressions (e.g., π2). *For example, by truncating the decimal expansion of √2, show that √2 is between 1 and 2, then between 1.4 and 1.5, and explain how to continue on to get better approximations.*			
Expressions and Equations			
CC.8.EE.1 Know and apply the properties of integer exponents to generate equivalent numerical expressions. *For example,* $3^2 \times 3^{-5} = 3^{-3} = 1/3^3 = 1/27.$	**Example:** *I can work with radicals and integer exponents.*		
CC.8.EE.2 Use square root and cube root symbols to represent solutions to equations of the form $x^2 = p$ and $x^3 = p$, where p is a positive rational number. Evaluate square roots of small perfect squares and cube roots of small perfect cubes. Know that √2 is irrational.			

From *Common Core State Standards for Mathematics*. Copyright © 2010.
National Governors Association Center for Best Practices and Council of Chief State School Officers. All rights reserved.

*NOTE: This is just one sample excerpt; the full collection of all Math standards at all grade levels is included in the digital download. See page ix for instructions on how to access.

Chapter 4
Meeting the Expectations of the Common Core

Although the Common Core State Standards (CCSS) do not endorse any one particular instructional strategy, tool, or program, I believe that strong student-centered instructional practices will lead to the development of CCSS skills. The CCSS make strong statements about students developing independence as they develop skills:

- They demonstrate independence.

- They build strong content knowledge.

- They respond to the varying demands of audience, task, purpose, and discipline.

- They comprehend as well as critique.

- They value evidence.

- They use technology and digital media strategically and capably.

- They come to understand other perspectives and cultures.

In order to build these college and career ready skills, students must engage in classroom practices that foster independent learning and thinking. The following five tools are designed to support your understanding and application of both a CCSS student-centered focus and instructional practices such as project-based learning, developing essential questions, argumentation in writing, and conducting research.

Note: While I address only a handful of specific teaching strategies in this book—Bloom's Taxonomy, differentiated instruction, student-centered learning, project-based learning, and Understanding by Design (UBD)—many other teaching models and methodologies can also be used to meet the expectations of the CCSS, such as Six Traits Writing, design thinking, inquiry-based learning, and online learning, to name a few. Unfortunately, I do not have the capacity here to address all of them. However, if you're already using a particular model that is working well for you, consider simple adjustments you can make to adapt it to the Common Core. Feel free to contact me if you'd like to discuss further.

TOOL #21: STUDENT-CENTERED LEARNING

According to Yale professor Harold Bloom, the greatest level of comprehension and understanding comes when students can represent what they know and understand. When you implement student-centered practices in the classroom, you create the context for students to engage in the higher-level thinking that the CCSS require. This focus is represented in **Figures 4.1 and 4.2** with statements from the standards for English language arts (ELA) and for mathematics. Notice how the bolded headings in the ELA standards pinpoint student performance and skill level.

FIGURE 4.1:
STUDENT-
CENTERED
FOCUS IN THE
ELA CCSS

Students Who Are College and Career Ready in Reading, Writing, Speaking, Listening, and Language

The descriptions that follow are not standards themselves but instead offer a portrait of students who meet the standards set out in this document. As students advance through the grades and master the standards in reading, writing, speaking, listening, and language, they are able to exhibit with increasing fullness and regularity these capacities of the literate individual.

They demonstrate independence.

Students can, without significant scaffolding, comprehend and evaluate complex texts across a range of types and disciplines, and they can construct effective arguments and convey intricate or multifaceted information. Likewise, students are able independently to discern a speaker's key points, request clarification, and ask relevant questions. They build on others' ideas, articulate their own ideas, and confirm they have been understood. Without prompting, they demonstrate command of standard English and acquire and use a wide-ranging vocabulary. More broadly, they become self-directed learners, effectively seeking out and using resources to assist them, including teachers, peers, and print and digital reference materials.

They build strong content knowledge.

Students establish a base of knowledge across a wide range of subject matter by engaging with works of quality and substance. They become proficient in new areas through research and study. They read purposefully and listen attentively to gain both general knowledge and discipline-specific expertise. They refine and share their knowledge through writing and speaking.

They respond to the varying demands of audience, task, purpose, and discipline.

Students adapt their communication in relation to audience, task, purpose, and discipline. They set and adjust purpose for reading, writing, speaking, listening, and language use as warranted by the task. They appreciate nuances, such as how the composition of an audience should affect tone when speaking and how the connotations of words affect meaning. They also know that different disciplines call for different types of evidence (e.g., documentary evidence in history, experimental evidence in science).

They comprehend as well as critique.

Students are engaged and open-minded—but discerning—readers and listeners. They work diligently to understand precisely what an author or speaker is saying, but they also question an author's or speaker's assumptions and premises and assess the veracity of claims and the soundness of reasoning.

They value evidence.

Students cite specific evidence when offering an oral or written interpretation of a text. They use relevant evidence when supporting their own points in writing and speaking, making their reasoning clear to the reader or listener, and they constructively evaluate others' use of evidence.

They use technology and digital media strategically and capably.

Students employ technology thoughtfully to enhance their reading, writing, speaking, listening, and language use. They tailor their searches online to acquire useful information efficiently, and they integrate what they learn using technology with what they learn offline. They are familiar with the strengths and limitations of various technological tools and mediums and can select and use those best suited to their communication goals.

They come to understand other perspectives and cultures.

Students appreciate that the twenty-first-century classroom and workplace are settings in which people from often widely divergent cultures and who represent diverse experiences and perspectives must learn and work together. Students actively seek to understand other perspectives and cultures through reading and listening, and they are able to communicate effectively with people of varied backgrounds. They evaluate other points of view critically and constructively. Through reading great classic and contemporary works of literature representative of a variety of periods, cultures, and worldviews, students can vicariously inhabit worlds and have experiences much different than their own.

From *Common Core State Standards for English Language Arts & Literacy in History/Social Studies, Science, and Technical Subjects,* p. 7. Copyright © 2010. National Governors Association Center for Best Practices and Council of Chief State School Officers. All rights reserved.

The Standards set grade-specific standards but do not define the intervention methods or materials necessary to support students who are well below or well above grade-level expectations. It is also beyond the scope of the Standards to define the full range of supports appropriate for English language learners and for students with special needs. At the same time, all students must have the opportunity to learn and meet the same high standards if they are to access the knowledge and skills necessary in their post-school lives. The Standards should be read as allowing for the widest possible range of students to participate fully from the outset, along with appropriate accommodations to ensure maximum participaton of students with special education needs. For example, for students with disabilities reading should allow for use of Braille, screen reader technology, or other assistive devices, while writing should include the use of a scribe, computer, or speech-to-text technology. In a similar vein, speaking and listening should be interpreted broadly to include sign language. No set of grade-specific standards can fully reflect the great variety in abilities, needs, learning rates, and achievement levels of students in any given classroom. However, the Standards do provide clear signposts along the way to the goal of college and career readiness for all students.

Tool #21 (**page 69 and Figure 4.3**) provides a checklist to help you make sure you are placing students at the center of your curriculum and instruction. This checklist is a powerful tool for teacher self-reflection. Consider using it at the end of every day. Take five minutes to assess your daily achievement by asking yourself, "Did my classroom demonstrate this expectation of student-centered education today?" Then check off each item that you believe you successfully accomplished. Write "working on" next to those goals that you attempted, but didn't quite complete. And write "N/A" by those goals that were not applicable to that particular day. (For example, the first goal, *Students' ideas and questions are welcomed, valued, and encouraged*, will be applicable every single day. But the goal, *Student input is sought in planning subject revision*, isn't likely to come up except at the end of a unit.) Leave goals unchecked if you didn't attempt them in your classroom on that day.

Review your self-reflection checklists every week or two. If you discover a pattern, strive to remedy it. If you notice that a goal is unchecked or marked "working on" for a number of days in a row, focus attention on that goal until it becomes part of your classroom routine. There's no right or wrong way to attain a student-centered classroom, and there are many effective techniques. So don't be shy about asking other teachers for suggestions about how to achieve expectations that don't come naturally to you.

EXAMPLE TOOL #21: STUDENT-CENTERED LEARNING

Attitude

☐ Students' ideas and questions are welcomed, valued, and encouraged.

☐ Students are seen as partners in a learning journey.

☐ Students are supported when they take responsibility for their own learning.

☐ Staff members have a commitment and desire to share their field of expertise and its relevance to professional practice.

☐ Staff members actively search for new ways to help students learn. Staff learn about teaching from evaluating and reflecting on student learning.

☐ Learning is fun and vital to personal development for grasping opportunities throughout life.

These elements create democratic and generative classrooms.

Communication

☐ Formal communications (subject guides, learning outcomes, assessment guidelines, timetables, etc.) are clear, specific, and in writing. (This includes any changes to the original information.)

☐ Discussion of aims and intentions include differing perspectives.

☐ Students receive timely and adequate information on which they can base assignment and study plans and decisions.

☐ Students are offered opportunities to discuss connections they are making with previous classes and other subjects in the course.

☐ Students' experiences and views about the school's programs are actively sought and used as an integral part of planning for future programs

Offer students multiple opportunities to work in collaborative groups to foster greater independence

Program/Subject Design

☐ Student input is sought in planning subject revision.

☐ Programs facilitate student choice, providing negotiation of learning outcomes where appropriate, and student adaptation of learning issues and context where possible.

☐ The planning of all aspects of programs involves students, to ensure their perspectives, ideas, and needs have been accommodated.

Clearly communicating expectations is critical to successful student-centered learning.

CONTINUED ON NEXT PAGE

Evaluation

☐ Students are offered opportunities to give feedback, with the assurance that issues will be addressed in response to that feedback.

☐ Staff members reflect on student feedback and performance, seeking improvement and adding documentation in personal teaching portfolios.

Notice that these qualities are also principles of formative assessment.

Learning Activities

☐ Prior learning is considered and discussed, addressing the needs of students who may be at different starting points.

☐ Learning activities are negotiated (when appropriate and possible), so that they occur in ways that students find relevant, engaging, and suitably challenging, thereby ensuring the development of high-school-graduate capabilities.

☐ A range of teaching methods is offered that will ensure the development of the necessary skills to meet the demands of industry and professional workplaces.

☐ Students with less effective processes are exposed to learners with more effective processes, thus creating a forum for sharing learning approaches and ideas.

☐ Opportunities are generated for students to explore their own hypotheses, promoting scholarly and reflective practices consistent with skill development as lifelong learners.

The learning activities also embody differentiated instruction principles.

Assessment Activities

☐ Staff explains assessment methods and negotiates where possible.

☐ Staff checks to ensure that the assessment achieves the desired high-school-graduate capabilities and requirements of professional practice in each discipline.

☐ A range of assessment approaches is made available to accommodate different learning styles.

☐ Opportunities are sought for both formal and informal peer and self-assessment.

TOOL #21 STUDENT-CENTERED LEARNING

Attitude

- ☐ Students' ideas and questions are welcomed, valued, and encouraged.
- ☐ Students are seen as partners in a learning journey.
- ☐ Students are supported when they take responsibility for their own learning.
- ☐ Staff members have a commitment and desire to share their field of expertise and its relevance to professional practice.
- ☐ Staff members actively search for new ways to help students learn. Staff learn about teaching from evaluating and reflecting on student learning.
- ☐ Learning is fun and vital to personal development for grasping opportunities throughout life.

Communication

- ☐ Formal communications (subject guides, learning outcomes, assessment guidelines, timetables, etc.) are clear, specific, and in writing. (This includes any changes to the original information.)
- ☐ Discussion of aims and intentions include differing perspectives.
- ☐ Students receive timely and adequate information on which they can base assignment and study plans and decisions.
- ☐ Students are offered opportunities to discuss connections they are making with previous classes and other subjects in the course.
- ☐ Students' experiences and views about the school's programs are actively sought and used as an integral part of planning for future programs

Program/Subject Design

- ☐ Student input is sought in planning subject revision.
- ☐ Programs facilitate student choice, providing negotiation of learning outcomes where appropriate, and student adaptation of learning issues and context where possible.
- ☐ The planning of all aspects of programs involves students, to ensure their perspectives, ideas, and needs have been accommodated.

Evaluation

- ☐ Students are offered opportunities to give feedback, with the assurance that issues will be addressed in response to that feedback.
- ☐ Staff members reflect on student feedback and performance, seeking improvement and adding documentation in personal teaching portfolios.

Learning Activities

- ☐ Prior learning is considered and discussed, addressing the needs of students who may be at different starting points.
- ☐ Learning activities are negotiated (when appropriate and possible), so that they occur in ways that students find relevant, engaging, and suitably challenging, thereby ensuring the development of high-school-graduate capabilities.
- ☐ A range of teaching methods is offered that will ensure the development of the necessary skills to meet the demands of industry and professional workplaces.
- ☐ Students with less effective processes are exposed to learners with more effective processes, thus creating a forum for sharing learning approaches and ideas.
- ☐ Opportunities are generated for students to explore their own hypotheses, promoting scholarly and reflective practices consistent with skill development as lifelong learners.

Assessment Activities

- ☐ Staff explains assessment methods and negotiates where possible.
- ☐ Staff checks to ensure that the assessment achieves the desired high-school-graduate capabilities and requirements of professional practice in each discipline.
- ☐ A range of assessment approaches is made available to accommodate different learning styles.
- ☐ Opportunities are sought for both formal and informal peer and self-assessment.

TOOL #22: PROJECT-BASED LEARNING 101

As you study the Common Core State Standards, you have probably already noticed that students are expected to demonstrate what they know and understand. Project-based learning (PBL) is an effective instructional strategy for students to synthesize skills and content knowledge. Projects demand rigor and maximum cognition of content in order to create a product that represents an individual student's learning.

What is PBL?

Briefly, PBL is an instructional strategy that focuses on a great driving question—an "essential question"— or problem statement that encourages students to explore. The essential question or problem statement for the project should encompass all project content and outcomes. It should also provide a central focus for student inquiry. Be sure you pose an authentic problem or significant question that engages students and requires core subject knowledge to solve. (See Tool #23 on page 73 for more on essential questions.)

Tool #22 (**page 72 and Figure 4.4**) is designed to help you incorporate PBL as you implement the Common Core. As the students explore a question or problem, create activities that develop the content knowledge and the skills that students need to meet a performance objective. The performance objective is comprised of what students know and are able to do as a result of the project-based learning experience.

Here are some of my favorite resources for project-based learning:

West Virginia State Board of Education (**wvde.state.wv.us/teach21/ pbl.html**) has an outstanding resource on project-based learning that includes examples for many disciplines and grade levels, as well as templates for planning and assessment.

Edutopia (**edutopia.org/project-based-learning**) also has some great PBL information and sample exemplary projects.

Buck Institute for Education has an entire website, *PBL-Online* (**bie.org/tools/online_resources/pbl-online**), dedicated to project-based learning that includes resources for supporting research for PBL, blog posts connecting CCSS to PBL, and a large project library.

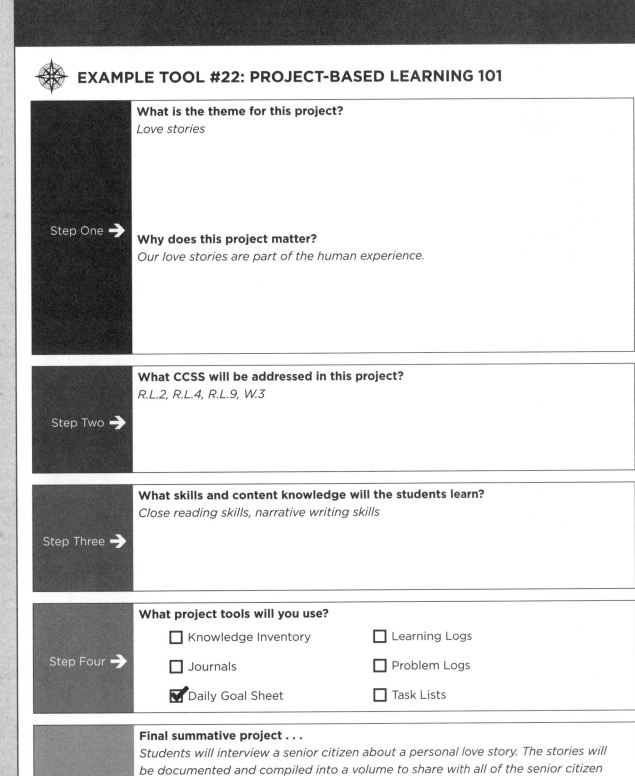

EXAMPLE TOOL #22: PROJECT-BASED LEARNING 101

Step One →

What is the theme for this project?
Love stories

Why does this project matter?
Our love stories are part of the human experience.

Step Two →

What CCSS will be addressed in this project?
R.L.2, R.L.4, R.L.9, W.3

Step Three →

What skills and content knowledge will the students learn?
Close reading skills, narrative writing skills

Step Four →

What project tools will you use?

☐ Knowledge Inventory   ☐ Learning Logs

☐ Journals   ☐ Problem Logs

☑ Daily Goal Sheet   ☐ Task Lists

Step Five →

Final summative project . . .
Students will interview a senior citizen about a personal love story. The stories will be documented and compiled into a volume to share with all of the senior citizen participants and student writers.

TOOL #22   PROJECT-BASED LEARNING 101

Step One →

What is the theme for this project?

Why does this project matter?

Step Two →

What CCSS will be addressed in this project?

Step Three →

What skills and content knowledge will the students learn?

Step Four →

What project tools will you use?

☐ Knowledge Inventory   ☐ Learning Logs

☐ Journals   ☐ Problem Logs

☐ Daily Goal Sheet   ☐ Task Lists

Step Five →

Final summative project . . .

TOOL #23: WRITING GREAT ESSENTIAL QUESTIONS

It makes sense to use essential questions as a curriculum focus for CCSS-aligned units. If you search the Internet, you'll find many CCSS curriculum maps that have used elements such as essential questions from Understanding by Design. Using essential questions for a CCSS-aligned curriculum is effective for the following reasons:

1. Common Core focuses on *skills* so that students can demonstrate what they know and understand. An essential question creates the focus for this to occur by offering students one specific question to address.

2. Great essential questions motivate students to go beyond "what" (basic content knowledge) to "how" and "why."

3. Often, in addressing an essential question, students will need to develop an argument. Argumentation is considered a foundational skill and is featured prominently in the CCSS. A student's ability to create a cogent argument is a key indicator of college and career readiness.

Developing a Great Essential Question

I'll be honest: I often struggle when I'm developing essential questions. Like many teachers, I frequently have to go back and revise my questions many times before I get them right. I've learned a little along the way about the pitfalls of constructing essential questions. When I teach educators about essential questions, I offer these two criteria:

1. If the drafted essential question can be answered using an online resource like Wikipedia, it's probably not an essential question. Those types of questions usually belong on the knowledge level of Bloom's Taxonomy and take the form of a "what" question.

2. The question must be provocative. Students have to be interested in answering the question.

Since the introduction of the CCSS, I've seen quite a few of what I like to refer to as "*faux*ssential questions." Following is an example of a *faux*ssential question paired with what I would consider to be an essential question.

Example:
What are the different shapes that a student can identify?

This is not an essential question because it does not go beyond the most fundamental level of understanding about shapes. Prior to kindergarten, most children can identify shapes because they've watched programs like *Barney* and *Sesame Street.*

A more rigorous essential question might be:
How do shapes help us understand and describe the world around us?

This is an essential question because it goes beyond a basic understanding of shapes. To address this question, students need to first be able to identify and understand shapes. Next, building on this basic knowledge, students need to apply this knowledge to a specific context.

The previous *faux*ssential question was one that I pulled from a state education website where it was provided as an essential question example for teachers. This leads me to an important caution: State education websites are providing many fabulous CCSS resources; however, in their rush to offer materials, they include some poor examples and misguided advice. Some of these websites contain incorrect information and perpetuate the myths I discussed in the introduction to this book.

Now that you have some background about essential questions, let's create some using Tool #23 (**page 76 and Figure 4.5**).

EXAMPLE TOOL #23: WRITING GREAT ESSENTIAL QUESTIONS

Use the following checklist to guide your writing of an essential question.

Question to Examine:
Can students identify different shapes?

It's not an essential question if . . .

☑ it can be answered "yes" or "no"

☐ it can be answered in one sentence

It may be an essential question if it . . .

☐ guides research

☑ is clear, concise, and coherent

☐ has no "right" answer

☐ promotes exploration and inquiry

☑ uses words like *what effect, why, if,* and *can*

Verdict:
This isn't an essential question since it doesn't promote analysis and critical thinking

Revised Question (if needed):
How do different shapes help me describe and understand my surroundings?

Use the following checklist to guide your writing of an essential question.

Question to Examine:

It's not an essential question if . . .

☐ it can be answered "yes" or "no"

☐ it can be answered in one sentence

It may be an essential question if it . . .

☐ guides research

☐ is clear, concise, and coherent

☐ has no "right" answer

☐ promotes exploration and inquiry

☐ uses words like *what effect, why, if,* and *can*

Verdict:

Revised Question (if needed):

TOOL #24: BASICS OF ARGUMENTATION

A foundational feature of the English language arts standards and the interdisciplinary literacy standards (applicable to *all* content area teachers) is Writing Standard 1: "Write arguments to support claims in an analysis of substantive topics or texts, using valid reasoning and relevant and sufficient evidence." Teachers in all subject areas need to teach students how to:

1. Write a claim

2. Provide evidence of the claim

3. Explain how the evidence supports the claim

Tool #24 (**page 79 and Figure 4.6**) is intended to help you meet this standard. Also, Appendix C of the CCSS is solely dedicated to the explanation and development of this standard; I urge you to examine the CCSS's Appendix C. It contains valuable information to help you understand the expectations of Writing Standard 1 at all grade levels.

EXAMPLE TOOL #24: BASICS OF ARGUMENTATION—MATH

CCSS W.1. Write arguments to support claims in an analysis of substantive topics or texts, using valid reasoning and relevant and sufficient evidence.

CLAIM (an opinion or assertion)

Statistics convey more than one story.

EVIDENCE (How are you proving your claim?)

Using a set of statistical data, explain how the data can tell more than one story.

REASONING (How does the evidence prove your claim?)

Using the statistical data, connect the different stories back to the claim.

CCSS W.1. Write arguments to support claims in an analysis of substantive topics or texts, using valid reasoning and relevant and sufficient evidence.

CLAIM (an opinion or assertion)

EVIDENCE (How are you proving your claim?)

REASONING (How does the evidence prove your claim?)

TOOL #25: EVALUATING ONLINE RESOURCES

Since every Internet search offers a staggering number of results, both teachers and students need to develop skills to evaluate the value of online resources. As you know, many Web-based resources are not useful or reliable. You must be able to help students figure out what is of value before they can begin to use retrieved information to expand their content knowledge.

The Common Core State Standards emphasize the importance of using a wide variety of resources, both print and electronic. Specifically, the following anchor standards articulate this expectation.

> **College and Career Readiness Anchor Standards for Reading:[1]**
> **7.** Integrate and evaluate content presented in diverse media and formats, including visually and quantitatively, as well as in words.
>
> **College and Career Readiness Anchor Standards for Writing:[2]**
> **6.** Use technology, including the Internet, to produce and publish writing and to interact and collaborate with others.
>
> **College and Career Readiness Anchor Standards for Speaking and Listening:[3]**
> **2.** Integrate and evaluate information presented in diverse media and formats, including visually, quantitatively, and orally.
> **5.** Make strategic use of digital media and visual displays of data to express information and enhance understanding of presentations.

In mathematics, the standards often advise using information that is collected from technological resources. The math standards also recommend technological tools both to create models and to use for problem solving.

Tool #25 (**page 82 and Figure 4.7**) will help you evaluate resources that you can use to meet some of the standards' technological expectations. You might consider adapting this tool to share with your students, as well.

---

[1] Common Core State Standards for English Language Arts & Literacy in History/ Social Studies, Science, and Technical Subjects, p. 10.
[2] Ibid., p. 18.
[3] Ibid., p. 22.

EXAMPLE TOOL #25: EVALUATING ONLINE RESOURCES

Title of Website: *Vocabulary/Spelling City*

Website Address: *www.spellingcity.com*

Authorship and Affiliations

☑ The website clearly indicates who the author is and what organization he or she is affiliated with.

☑ The author or organization appears reputable and knowledgeable about the website topic.

☑ The website clearly states when the information was edited or published.

Sources and Quotations

☐ Direct quotes are clearly marked and identified.

☑ External sources of information are cited.

Notes:

I could use this site with my first grade students in a learning center. Many of the activities can be self-directed to increase student independence.

Title of Website:

Website Address:

Authorship and Affiliations

- [ ] The website clearly indicates who the author is and what organization he or she is affiliated with.
- [ ] The author or organization appears reputable and knowledgeable about the website topic.
- [ ] The website clearly states when the information was edited or published.

Sources and Quotations

- [ ] Direct quotes are clearly marked and identified.
- [ ] External sources of information are cited.

Notes:

Chapter 5

Addressing Text Complexity and Vocabulary

Substantial mythology surrounds text complexity and academic vocabulary in the Common Core State Standards (CCSS). Gaining a clear understanding of the elements of the CCSS textual model is essential to developing an aligned curriculum. The four tools in this chapter will help you gain that understanding.

TOOL #26: WHAT IS TEXT COMPLEXITY?

Text complexity, according to the Common Core State Standards, contains the following three components:

1. **Quantitative measures.** These factors are difficult or impossible for a person to evaluate efficiently. They are typically measured by computer software. Examples include word length or frequency, sentence length, and text cohesion. The CCSS document uses Lexile measures to determine the quantitative aspects of a text.

2. **Qualitative measures.** These characteristics must be evaluated by a teacher. They include levels of meaning (literary texts) or purpose (informational texts), structure, language conventionality and clarity, and knowledge demands.

3. **Reader considerations.** This component also is best evaluated by a teacher who understands the students. It includes assessing the reader's motivation, knowledge, and experiences, as well as the purpose and complexity of a text.

Tool #26 (**page 85 and Figure 5.1**) clearly defines this three-part textual complexity model. The tool is designed to facilitate the construction of a reading list that meets what the CCSS refers to as a "staircase of complexity." Students need to read a wide variety of texts that have been selected based on these three components in order to develop skills, comprehension, and close-reading ability for college and career readiness. I strongly urge you to look at the appendices in the English language arts (ELA) standards for extensive information regarding text complexity. Note that quantitative measures are only one-third of the total model for text complexity. The other two-thirds of the model depend on the professional expertise of the teacher to determine if a text is challenging for a particular student. The rubric on **page 91** accompanies Tool #26 and is designed to help you assess qualitative measures for informational texts.

✴ EXAMPLE TOOL #26: WHAT IS TEXT COMPLEXITY?

Text Title	Quantitative Measures (word length, word frequency, word difficulty, and sentence length, e.g., Lexiles)	Qualitative Measures (levels of meaning or inference, levels of purpose, structure, organization, language conventionality, language clarity, and prior knowledge demands; e.g., rubrics)	Reader and Task Considerations (student motivation, knowledge, and experience; purpose for reading; complexity of the task assigned; and complexity of questions regarding the text; e.g., teacher checklist)			
To Kill a Mockingbird	Fifth grade according to Lexile	Due to complex themes and background knowledge demands, the text should be placed between seventh and ninth grade.	This is an assigned text for the students to read.			
Charlotte's Web	Fourth grade according to Lexile	Interest level is third to sixth grade and contains the following themes: death, grief, loss, friends and friendship, farm and ranch life.	The students may choose this text in a guided reading program. Choice should result in greater motivation for reading.			

TOOL #26

WHAT IS TEXT COMPLEXITY?

Text Title	Quantitative Measures (word length, word frequency, word difficulty, and sentence length, e.g., Lexiles)	Qualitative Measures (levels of meaning or inference, levels of purpose, structure, organization, language conventionality, language clarity, and prior knowledge demands; e.g., rubrics)	Reader and Task Considerations (student motivation, knowledge, and experience; purpose for reading; complexity of the task assigned; and complexity of questions regarding the text; e.g., teacher checklist)

TOOL #27: CONSTRUCTING A READING LIST THAT BUILDS TEXT COMPLEXITY

As discussed in Tool #26, the Common Core State Standards promote a reading curriculum that facilitates students to advance in a staircase of text complexity throughout their education. The model for text complexity includes quantitative measures, qualitative measures, and reader and task considerations, as indicated in Tool #27 (**page 88 and Figure 5.2**). The new standards also emphasize the role of informational text coupled with literary text. As teachers, we need to consider these variables in building a reading curriculum. Our goal, ultimately, is to lead students to the achievement of Reading Anchor Standard 10: "Read and comprehend complex literary and informational texts independently and proficiently."

Note in Figure 5.2 how the texts are not arranged simply in ascending order based on Lexile scores. Instead, the order factors in their teacher-determined qualitative dimensions and reader and task considerations.

EXAMPLE TOOL #27: CONSTRUCTING A READING LIST THAT BUILDS TEXT COMPLEXITY

Grade Level and Purpose: *Fourth grade books for literature circle on friendship*

Text Title	Quantitative Measures	Qualitative Dimensions	Reader and Task Considerations
Charlotte's Web	690 (Lexile)	friendship, death, loss	lit circle*
Stuart Little	920 (Lexile)	family, friendship, creativity	lit circle*
Matilda	840 (Lexile)	creativity, relationships	lit circle*
Tom Sawyer	950 (Lexile)	friendship, creativity	higher level; male protagonist
The Invention of Hugo Cabret	820 (Lexile)	relationships, creativity	lit circle; male protagonist

LOWER LEVEL →

CHALLENGING READ →

*Remember, students choose the book in a lit circle.

CONSTRUCTING A READING LIST THAT BUILDS TEXT COMPLEXITY

Grade Level and Purpose:

Text Title	Quantitative Measures	Qualitative Dimensions	Reader and Task Considerations

TOOLS #28-30: ACADEMIC VOCABULARY

The CCSS address vocabulary as part of the language strand of the English language arts standards. The College and Career Readiness Anchor Standards also articulate expectations of what students should be able to do with academic vocabulary. Specifically:

Reading Anchor Standard 4 expects students to interpret technical, connotative, and figurative meanings of words and phrases. In addition, this standard also establishes the expectation that students can analyze how specific word choices shape meaning or tone.

Language Anchor Standard 4 focuses on the student's ability to determine or clarify the meaning of unknown and multiple meaning words and phrases by using context clues, by analyzing meaningful word parts, and by consulting reference materials.

Language Anchor Standard 5 establishes the expectation that students can demonstrate understanding of figurative language, word relationships, and nuances in word meanings.

Language Anchor Standard 6 expects students to be able to acquire and accurately use a range of general academic and domain specific words and phrases. Additionally, students should demonstrate independence in gathering vocabulary knowledge when encountering an unknown term.

Without a growing familiarity with academic vocabulary, students have a difficult time acquiring more advanced conceptual knowledge. Generally, academic language is divided into three tiers, as described in the language strand of the English language arts Common Core State Standards:

Tier one words are common words acquired in the early grades and through everyday speech. Tier one words typically don't have multiple meanings.

Tier two words are high-frequency words used across several content areas. Tier two words present challenges to students, because they are not as common as tier one words and their meaning can change, depending on the context.

Tier three words are content-specific. Central to building knowledge and conceptual understanding, tier three words support understanding in academic domains and are critical to the instruction of specific content or subjects.

The following three tools (**pages 92–94**) provide sample key words at each of these tiers. Refer to these wordlists when planning curriculum aligned with the Common Core.

When planning, specifically teach the tiered words through activities such as vocabulary slides, concept sorts, or games. The idea is to directly teach the vocabulary and provide opportunities for students to practice using the words.

Here are some resources for teaching vocabulary:

Carleton, Lindsay, and Robert J. Marzano. *Vocabulary Games for the Classroom.* Bloomington, IN: Marzano Research Laboratory, 2010.

Freeman, Yvonne S., and David E. Freeman. *Academic Language for English Language Learners and Struggling Readers: How to Help Students Succeed Across Content Areas.* Portsmouth, NH: Heinemann, 2009.

McKnight, Katherine S. *The Elementary Teacher's Big Book of Graphic Organizers: 100 Ready-to-Use Organizers That Help Kids Learn Language Arts, Science, Social Studies, and More!* San Francisco, CA: Jossey-Bass, 2013.

RUBRIC   DETERMINING QUALITATIVE MEASURES FOR INFORMATIONAL TEXTS

Directions: Use the following rubric to assess the complexity of an informational text and determine its qualitative measures.

	Highest Complexity	Higher Complexity	Moderately Complex	Low Complexity
TEXT STRUCTURE	**Organization:** intricate or discipline-specific **Text Features** (if used): essential for content comprehension **Graphics:** may provide information not otherwise conveyed in the text	**Organization:** may contain multiple pathways or exhibit some discipline-specific traits **Text Features** (if used): enhance content comprehension **Graphics:** may support or be integral to understanding the text	**Organization:** clear and generally sequential or chronological **Text Features** (if used): enhance content comprehension **Graphics:** generally supplementary to understanding the text	**Organization:** chronological, sequential, or easy to predict **Text Features** (if used): help the reader navigate and understand content, but are not essential to understanding content **Graphics:** may assist readers in understanding the text
LANGUAGE FEATURES	**Conventionality of Text:** considerable abstract, ironic, or figurative language **Vocabulary:** generally unfamiliar, archaic, subject-specific, or overly academic language **Sentence Structure:** complex, with several subordinate clauses or phrases and transition words	**Conventionality of Text:** some abstract, ironic, or figurative language **Vocabulary:** sometimes unfamiliar, archaic, subject-specific, or overly academic **Sentence Structure:** may be complex, with several subordinate phrases or clauses and transition words	**Conventionality of Text:** explicit and easy to understand, with some occasions for more complex meaning **Vocabulary:** rarely overly academic **Sentence Structure:** mostly simple and compound sentences; may contain some complex constructions	**Conventionality of Text:** explicit, literal, straightforward, and easy to understand **Vocabulary:** generally contemporary, familiar, and conversational **Sentence Structure:** simple sentences
PURPOSE	**Purpose:** subtle and intricate, difficult to determine	**Purpose:** implicit or subtle but fairly easy to infer	**Purpose:** implied but easy to identify	**Purpose:** explicitly stated
KNOWLEDGE DEMANDS	**Subject Matter Knowledge:** relies on extensive levels of discipline-specific or theoretical knowledge **Intertextuality:** contains references or allusions to other texts or outside ideas	**Subject Matter Knowledge:** mixes recognizable ideas with challenging abstract concepts **Intertextuality:** contains references or allusions to other texts or outside ideas	**Subject Matter Knowledge:** relies on common practical knowledge and some discipline-specific content knowledge **Intertextuality:** contains references or allusions to other texts or outside ideas	**Subject Matter Knowledge:** includes simple, concrete ideas **Intertextuality:** contains references or allusions to other texts or outside ideas

Preschool

a, and, away, big, blue, can, come, down, find, for, funny, go, help, here, I , in, is, it, jump, little, look, make, me, my, not, one, play, red, run, said, see, the, three, to, two, up, we, where, yellow, you

Kindergarten

all, am, are, at, ate, be, black, brown, but, came, did, do, eat, four, get, good, have, he, into, like, must, new, no, now, on, our, out, please, pretty, ran, ride, saw, say, she, so, soon, that, there, they, this, too, under, want, was, well, went, what, white, who, will, with, yes

First Grade

after, again, an, any, as, ask, by, could, every, fly, from, give, going, had, has, her, him, his, how, just, know, let, live, may, of, old, once, open, over, put, round, some, stop, take, thank, them, then, think, walk, were, when

Second Grade

always, around, because, been, before, best, both, buy, call, cold, does, don't, fast, five, found, gave, goes, green, its, made, many, off, or, pull, read, right, sing, sit, sleep, tell, their, these, those, upon, us, use, very, wash, which, why, wish, work, would, write, your

Third Grade

about, better, bring, carry, clean, cut, done, draw, drink, eight, fall, far, full, got, grow, hold, hot, hurt, if, keep, kind, laugh, light, long, much, myself, never, only, own, pick, seven, shall, show, six, small, start, ten, today, together, try, warm

A–C

accelerate, achieve, adjacent, alternative, analyze, approach, approximate, arbitrary, assert, assess, assign, assume, authorize, automatic, chapter, compensate, complex, complicate, comply, component, comprehend, conceive, concentrate, concept, conclude, consequence, consist, constant, construct, consult, context, contrast, contribute, convert, create, criterion, crucial

D–F

data, define, definite, demonstrate, denote, derive, design, devise, devote, dimension, distinct, distort, element, emphasize, empirical, ensure, entity, environment, equate, equivalent, establish, evaluate, evident, expand, expose, external, feasible, fluctuate, focus, formulate, function

G–L

generate, guarantee, hypothesis, identify, ignore, illustrate, impact, implicit, imply, indicate, individual, inhibit, initial, innovation, intense, interpret, intuitive, involve, isolate

M–P

magnetic, magnitude, major, manipulate, mathematics, method, minimum, modify, negative, notion, obtain, obvious, occur, passive, period, perspective, pertinent, phase, phenomena, portion, potential, precede, precise, presume, prime, principle, proceed, publish, pursue

Q–S

random, range, react, region, require, respective, restrict, reverse, role, section, segment, select, sequence, series, shift, signify, similar, simultaneous, sophisticated, species, specify, stable, statistic, status, structure, subsequent, suffice, sum, summary

T–Z

technique, technology, tense, theory, trace, tradition, transmit, ultimate, undergo, usage, valid, vary, verbal, verify, vertical

Social Studies

abolitionist, alliance, amendment, bonds, budget, capital, capitalism, competition, Crusades, deflation, democracy, ecosystem, Enlightenment, federalism, genocide, humanism, immigration, investment, longitude, McCarthyism, nationalism, NATO, outsourcing, profit, referendum, Renaissance, sovereignty, urbanization, Warsaw Pact

English Language Arts

allegory, assonance, bias, characterization, consonance, digraph, fable, fantasy, fluency, genre, hyperbole, irony, lyric, metaphor, onomatopoeia, parody, plot, prose, repetition, sequencing, sonnet, suffix, testimonial, understatement

Science

adaptation, atmosphere, atom, biotic, catalyst, classify, constellation, data, deposition, dominant, DNA, environment, fertilization, force, friction, gravity, isotope, mass, mitosis, neutron, organic, pH, plate tectonics, proton, recessive, structure, theory, variable, vertebrate

Mathematics

addition, algorithm, annuity, approximation, area, base, calculation, coefficient, collinear, common factor, compute, denominator, exponent, formula, graph, intercept, line, logarithm, mode, numerator, parameter, postulate, quadrilateral, ray, scale, tangent, unit circle, weight, zero property

Chapter 6
Differentiating the Standards

The Common Core State Standards (CCSS) focus on skill development. Differentiated instruction (DI) offers a sound instructional approach to develop skills at different rates and through varied approaches for different individuals. Although, as I've said previously, the CCSS do not suggest or endorse any one particular instructional strategy or curriculum, differentiated instruction makes sense to support the CCSS expectations. The following five tools will help you and your colleagues think about how to incorporate differentiation as you create CCSS-aligned curriculum and instruction.

TOOL #31: ALIGNING DIFFERENTIATED INSTRUCTION (DI) WITH THE CCSS

Given CCSS expectations such as Reading Anchor Standard 10, "read and comprehend complex literary and informational texts independently and proficiently," how would we, as teachers, be able to meet this standard without differentiating the texts in reading tasks for individual students? Differentiated instruction is essential to maintaining fidelity to the standards. Tool #31 (**page 97 and Figure 6.1**) helps you determine how the DI strategies you use (or would like to use) support the CCSS framework.

EXAMPLE TOOL #31: ALIGNING DIFFERENTIATED INSTRUCTION (DI) WITH THE CCSS

DI Strategy	How DI Strategy Aligns with the CCSS
Multiple Levels of Questions [Questions are adjusted based on advanced problem solving skills. See resources such as Bloom's Taxonomy for developing leveled questions.]	*Leveled questions help students develop the sophisticated skills needed to pose the complex questions required by the new standards.*
Choice Boards [Choice boards and learning menus outline a variety of instructional options targeted to the learning goals.]	*Menus allow for different levels of ability, which is essential in meeting the skills articulated in the CCSS.*
Learning Centers [Learning centers can be "stations" that you set up, each with a different focused activity for students to explore content and develop skills.]	*Centers ensure that students are working at their ability level to allow for the continuous development of skills that are articulated in the CCSS anchor standards.*
Flexible Grouping [Students work as part of many different groups depending on the task or content and their readiness for each task or content topic.]	*Flexible grouping ensures rigor, a foundational feature of the CCSS.*
Anchor Activities [Enrichment activities that students can do by themselves if they finish work before their classmates.]	*Like flexible grouping, anchor activities promote rigor by having students work independently at their highest level.*
Tiered Assignments [Teachers create varied levels of activities to promote student exploration of ideas at a level that builds on prior knowledge and promotes continued growth.]	*Tiered assignments enable students to learn at their corresponding ability level, so they are working at a rigorous and independent level. These assignments also reinforce or extend concepts and principles based on student readiness—another CCSS premise.*

These sample DI strategies represent some of the most popular among numerous options.

The Introduction and Appendices of the CCSS document articulate many of the broad goals that DI strategies serve so well.

DI Strategy	How DI Strategy Aligns with the CCSS

TOOL #32: DIFFERENTIATED INSTRUCTION CHECKLIST

This tool (**page 99**) is a general checklist to keep track of how well your students are being served by the DI strategies you are using prior to and during instruction as you implement the Common Core State Standards. Not every item will be checked off for every lesson. Plan to focus on three or four goals at a time. Then, as time goes on, you'll find yourself routinely presenting rigorous, engaging lessons that promote high-level thinking. By paying special attention to the *Planning for Instruction* steps, you'll develop confidence and a skill set that empowers you to work with a variety of learners.

Directions: As a DI beginner, choose three to four items from this checklist as a primary focus.[1] As you become more comfortable and skilled, check off more items.

Planning for Instruction

☐ Are you being clear about the facts, information, and what students will be able to do as a result of the instruction?

☐ What resources do you need to implement the lessons?

☐ How will you pre-assess the students so you are able to accommodate their learning needs?

☐ Do all activities promote high-level thinking and rigor?

☐ Are activities interesting and engaging?

Notes:

During Instruction

☐ Is there variety in group assignments?

☐ Are students encouraged to "work up"?

☐ Are provisions made for students who prefer to work independently?

☐ Do students have choices for engaging activities?

☐ How will you gather assessment data?

Notes:

---

[1] Checklist adapted from Tomlinson, 1999; 2001; and 2003.

TOOL #33: CREATING DIFFERENTIATED TEXT SETS

The following scenario represents a familiar situation for many teachers:

Let's say, I'm an eighth grade social studies teacher. I have about twenty-five students in my class. According to reading comprehension tests, roughly five of my students are reading above level. Ten of my students are reading at what would be considered grade level. Of the remaining ten students, five are reading about one year below level and five are reading significantly below level. This presents a challenge. If I use my textbook (which is written at what would be considered grade level) as the primary source for reading material, I am clearly not meeting the reading needs of all my students.

What we know about reading is that teachers must meet students at their reading level if those students are to continue developing comprehension. An effective instructional tool both for improving reading skills and for developing content knowledge is text sets. Text sets are groups of materials selected because they meet the following criteria:

1. Each text in the set develops content knowledge.

2. The texts are varied in reading levels so they meet the diverse reading abilities of a class of students.

3. Every effort is made to use texts that will garner student interest.

Here's an example of a text set that includes a variety of articles and other reading materials to develop content knowledge:

Topic: Union and Confederate Soldiers During the Civil War

Associated Essential Question: What was the human cost of the Civil War for those who actually witnessed and participated in battle?

Possible Texts in the Set: Articles selected from websites such as the Smithsonian Institution, photographs from the Library of Congress website, letters written between soldiers and their families, and materials from references like *National Geographic* or Ken Burns's epic documentary on the Civil War.

Notice that the materials include written text, media, and online resources. This text set meets not only the reading needs of a diverse class, but also the CCSS expectation that students read and use a wide variety of increasingly complex texts (Reading Anchor Standard 10).

For a text set to be effective, you must assess students' varying needs on a consistent basis to ensure that the reading materials continue to push everyone's comprehension skills. As an individual student's abilities change, adjustments need to be made to ensure the reading materials are always at the appropriate level.

Tool #33 (**page 102 and Figure 6.2**) is a form for you to fill in as you plan differentiated text sets that provide all of your students with materials they can read. That will, in turn, effectively improve reading skills and develop content knowledge for every student in your class.

✶ EXAMPLE TOOL #33: CREATING DIFFERENTIATED TEXT SETS

Topic or Area of Study:
Biology: Environment and Survival Traits

This science text set targets seventh grade students who represent a wide variety of reading levels.

Essential Question:
How can a particular environment select traits for greater likelihood of survival and reproduction?

Essential questions are usually "how" or "why" questions and promote higher-level thinking with application and representation.

Texts

Low Level	Middle Level	High Level
Adapted from biology reference: www.biologyreference.com/Mo-Nu/Natural-Selection.html *Teacher edited to create simpler sentences and vocabulary.*	Adapted from *American Museum of Natural History*: www.amnh.org/education/resources/rfl/web/darwinguide/selection.html *Teacher edited to create simpler sentences and vocabulary.*	*"Climate Effects on Human Evolution,"* from National Museum of Natural History: humanorigins.si.edu/research/climate-research/effects

Since textbooks are generally written at one grade level, supplement them richly with an assortment that presents content at a variety of reading levels. Consider also using videos and other additional sources.

Topic or Area of Study:

Essential Question:

Texts			
Low Level	Middle Level	High Level	

TOOLS #34–35: ADAPTING THE STANDARDS

The next two tools serve to remind you that the Common Core State Standards are guidelines. They are designed to offer flexibility, and they require professional input and contextual adaptation in order to be usable. As indicated in the introduction to the CCSS document, teachers and curriculum specialists know best how students are going to develop the articulated skills. Tools #34 and #35 aim to streamline the process of differentiating the standards to meet specific needs for high-level learners.

Tool #34: Pump Up the Standard: Sophisticated Complexity

It's easy to neglect high-achieving students. They appear to be self-motivated because they frequently read copious amounts of material without prompting. But are they really challenging themselves? As a teacher, you can customize the CCSS to meet the specific needs of a high-level student. Tool #34 (**page 105 and Figure 6.3**) is designed to guide you through this customization process. In the *Standard* bubble at the top of the diagram, identify the standard and the skills a student needs to develop. For example, if you have a sixth grade student who is reading at an eighth grade level, you would include aspects of both the sixth and the eighth grade standards. In the *Up 1–2 in Bloom's* bubble, consider how you would differentiate the standard in order to accelerate student learning according to Bloom's Taxonomy levels. In the bubble labeled *Go into greater sophistication from this description*, record what specific strategies and learning targets you have designed for this particular student.

EXAMPLE TOOL #34: PUMP UP THE STANDARD: SOPHISTICATED COMPLEXITY

Reading Standard #3 for Informational Text as articulated for Grade 6

What's the procedural knowledge aspect?

Standard:
RI.6.3: Analyze in detail how a key individual, event, or idea is introduced, illustrated, and elaborated in a text (e.g., through examples or anecdotes).

Choose Option 1 or 2

Reading Standard #3 for Informational Text as articulated for Grades 7 and 8

Specific strategies and learning targets for this student.

Up 1–2 Levels in Bloom's Taxonomy
RI.7.3: Analyze the interactions between individuals, events, and ideas in a text (e.g., how ideas influence individuals or events, or how individuals influence ideas or events)

Go into greater sophistication from this description
Add National Geographic *article to global warming unit reading list.*
Encourage student to research using 3+ websites for Revolutionary War unit final essay. (Suggest History.com.)
Make sure student includes scientists, inventions, and practical applications on timeline/outline analysis project.
(Should be able to make connections between them.)

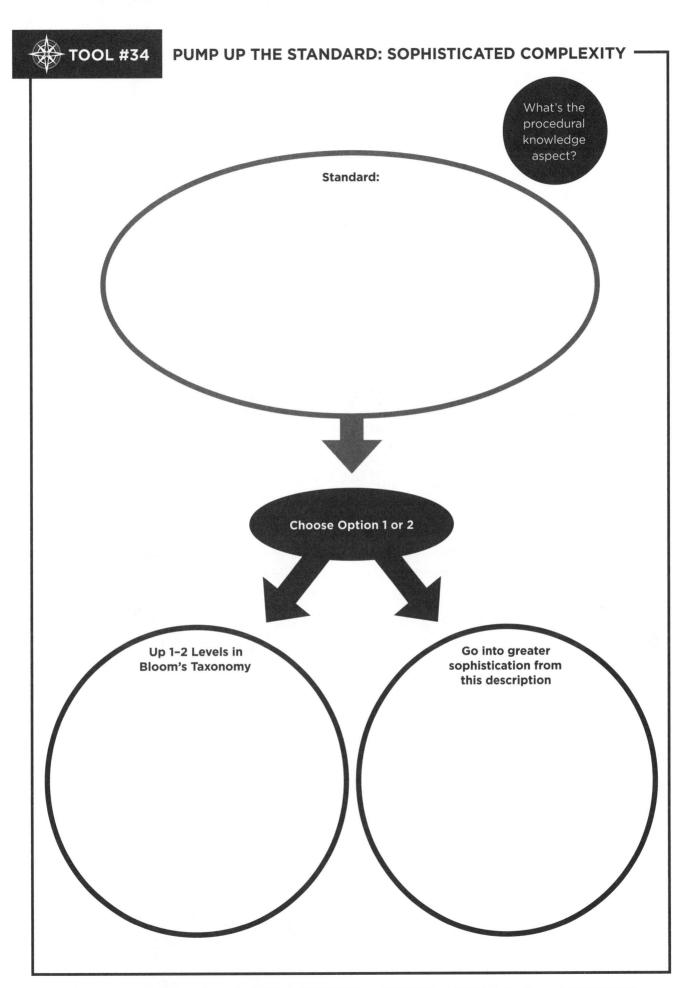

What's the procedural knowledge aspect?

Standard:

Choose Option 1 or 2

Up 1–2 Levels in Bloom's Taxonomy

Go into greater sophistication from this description

Tool #35: Ramp Up the Standard: Acceleration

Some teachers find that they have students who are ready for learning tasks at levels higher than their grade-level standards. These students need subject acceleration, which Tool #35 will help you plan. You'll notice that this tool (**page 108 and Figure 6.4**) has a recursive design. The first step is to look at the actual grade-level standards for a student. For example, if you have a third grade student who is reading at a fifth grade reading level, you record the third grade standards in the oval labeled, *Grade-Level Standard(s)*. Next, look at the fourth grade standards to determine the appropriateness of those standards for your accelerated third grader. Then proceed through the fifth, sixth, and seventh grade standards, as necessary, until you find the corresponding standards that meet the actual reading level of this student. Record the appropriate standards in the middle oval, *Accelerated Grade-Level Standard(s)*. In the final oval, *How is this accelerated standard addressing and building on the grade-level standard(s)*, list teaching methods and describe how they meet the individual learning needs of this particular student.

EXAMPLE TOOL #35: RAMP UP THE STANDARD: ACCELERATION

Reading Standard #1 for Literature as articulated for Grade 3

Grade-Level Standard(s)
RL.3.1: Ask and answer questions to demonstrate understanding of a text, referring explicitly to the text as the basis for the answers.

Accelerate to the next grade level.

Accelerated Grade-Level Standard(s)
RL.4.1: Refer to details and samples in a text when explaining what the text says explicitly and when drawing inferences from the text.

Reading Standard #1 for Literature as articulated for Grades 4 and 5

List needs and applicable teaching methods/strategies for this student

How is this accelerated standard addressing and building on the grade-level standard(s)?
Student will not only demonstrate understanding of text by referencing it, she'll refer to specific details and quote text to support her ideas. Teach student to use quotation marks when writing. Develop student's close reading skills by adding anticipation guide and story trails template to her "toolbox" folder.

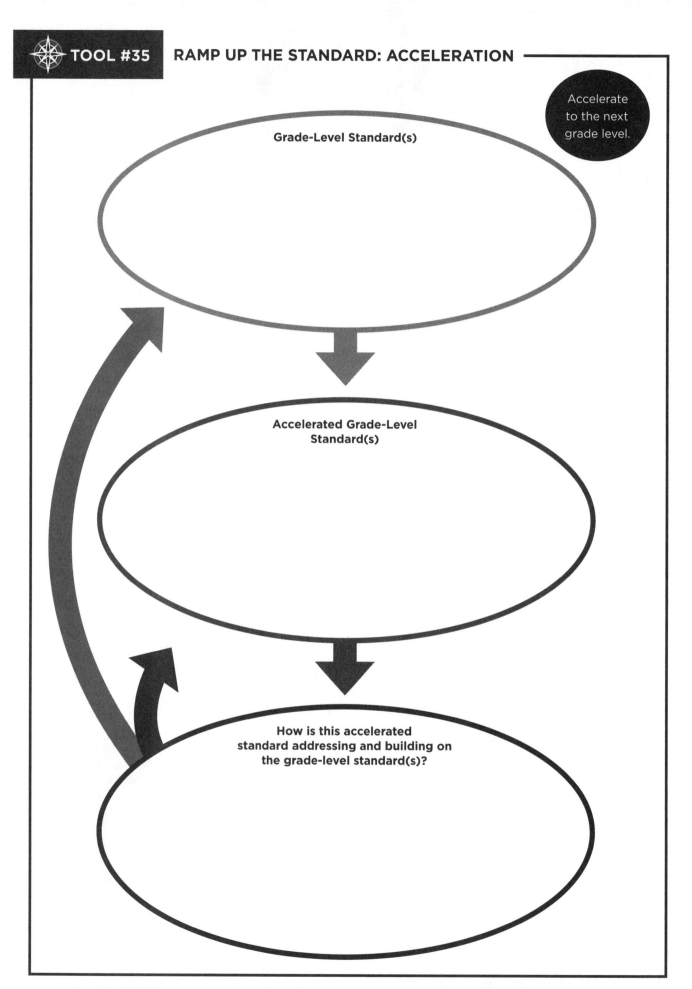

Accelerate to the next grade level.

Grade-Level Standard(s)

Accelerated Grade-Level Standard(s)

How is this accelerated standard addressing and building on the grade-level standard(s)?

Chapter 7
Schoolwide Common Core

In addition to my work with teacher colleagues, I also present to and teach administrators about the Common Core. Frequently, administrators will ask my advice about transitioning to the CCSS on a schoolwide level. The five planning tools in this chapter reflect my advice for a schoolwide transition, in addition to the information included in Tool #13 on page 47.

Once you have completed these five planning tools—a process that often takes longer than just one school year—the seeds for a successful transition will have been planted. Your school will be on its way toward curriculum and instruction that is more aligned with the expectations of the CCSS, and quality, research-based instruction will happen.

TOOL #36: PROFESSIONAL LEARNING COMMUNITY PLANNER

In order to transition successfully to the CCSS, teachers must have regular time to develop the curriculum and materials to meet the fidelity of the new standards. Provide teachers with regularly structured opportunities to work collaboratively and to address curriculum instruction and assessment issues. Professional learning communities (PLCs) offer a powerful way for educators to come together to discuss strategies and plans for curriculum and instruction within the school community. Tool #36 (**page 111 and Figure 7.1**) provides a template that is based on the tools in this book. It will assist you and the professional learning community (PLC) in creating a plan for the full academic year. The PLC Planner is designed for educators to plan for professional development and discussions.

EXAMPLE TOOL #36: PROFESSIONAL LEARNING COMMUNITY PLANNER

Tool #	Tool Name	Suggested Timeframe During the Year
1–2	Close Reading and Examination of the CCSS	Work in content-specific teams in the first month of school or during professional development days prior to the start of the school year. Extend to professional development days in October.
3–4	Foundational Features of the CCSS	
5	Understanding Academic Language in the CCSS	
6	Fulcrum and Focus Standards	
7	Identifying Paradigm Shifts	
8	Comparing the Standards in the CCSS	Conduct a series of professional learning community (PLC) meetings in November and December.
9	Gap Analysis	
10	Curriculum Audit	
11–12	Curriculum Strengths and Weaknesses	
13	Schoolwide Transition Plan	Begin in January in PLCs
14	Identifying Needs while Transitioning	
15–16	Mapping Curriculum	
17	Compatible Curriculum Design for the CCSS	
18–20	Sample Standards Matrices	
21	Student-Centered Learning	Begin in March in PLCs
22	Project-Based Learning 101	
23	Writing Great Essential Questions	
24	Basics of Argumentation	
25	Evaluating Online Resources	
26	What Is Text Complexity?	Summer professional development
27	Constructing a Reading List That Builds Text Complexity	
28–30	Academic Vocabulary	
31	Aligning Differentiated Instruction with the CCSS	Begin in Year 1; continue to Year 2
32	Differentiated Instruction Checklist	
33	Creating Differentiated Text Sets	
34	Pump Up the Standard: Sophisticated Complexity	
35	Ramp Up the Standard: Acceleration	
36	Professional Learning Community Planner	Begin in Year 1; continue to Year 2 Teacher committee with principal
37	School Technology Implementation Planner	
38	School Literacy Planner	
39	Formative Assessment Planner	
40	Master Assessment Schedule	

Tool #	Tool Name	Suggested Timeframe During the Year
1–2	Close Reading and Examination of the CCSS	
3–4	Foundational Features of the CCSS	
5	Understanding Academic Language in the CCSS	
6	Fulcrum and Focus Standards	
7	Identifying Paradigm Shifts	
8	Comparing the Standards in the CCSS	
9	Gap Analysis	
10	Curriculum Audit	
11–12	Curriculum Strengths and Weaknesses	
13	Schoolwide Transition Plan	
14	Identifying Needs while Transitioning	
15–16	Mapping Curriculum	
17	Compatible Curriculum Design for the CCSS	
18–20	Sample Standards Matrices	
21	Student-Centered Learning	
22	Project-Based Learning 101	
23	Writing Great Essential Questions	
24	Basics of Argumentation	
25	Evaluating Online Resources	
26	What Is Text Complexity?	
27	Constructing a Reading List That Builds Text Complexity	
28–30	Academic Vocabulary	
31	Aligning Differentiated Instruction with the CCSS	
32	Differentiated Instruction Checklist	
33	Creating Differentiated Text Sets	
34	Pump Up the Standard: Sophisticated Complexity	
35	Ramp Up the Standard: Acceleration	
36	Professional Learning Community Planner	
37	School Technology Implementation Planner	
38	School Literacy Planner	
39	Formative Assessment Planner	
40	Master Assessment Schedule	

TOOL #37: SCHOOL TECHNOLOGY IMPLEMENTATION PLANNER

Technological tools are crucial to twenty-first-century education. Making technology an integrated component of curriculum and instruction that leads to college and career readiness requires a plan as well as the acquisition of equipment and Internet access. Every school context is different; consequently, the integration of technology varies widely. Use Tool #37 (**page 114 and Figure 7.2**) to help you develop a plan to fully integrate technology into the teaching of content as well as to build literacy skills. This planner is comprised of two phases to facilitate the integration of technology into a school curriculum.

EXAMPLE TOOL #37: SCHOOL TECHNOLOGY IMPLEMENTATION PLANNER

Phase One

- Identify the decision makers (e.g., administration, committees, school board).

- Gather information about the current state of technology in your school or district.

- Develop a vision for technology and align to the CCSS.

- Plan a sequence of professional development that is differentiated to meet the needs of the teachers.

Ideas:
- ☑ Conduct teacher survey on technology needs.
- ☑ Analyze needs and resources.
- ☑ Establish technology vision, with collaborative effort from faculty and administration.
- ☑ Create PLC schedule.

Phase Two

- Provide continued support for technology implementation through professional learning communities (PLCs) and leadership teams.

- Include a variety of areas of expertise (e.g., special education, administration, ELL instruction).

Ideas:
- ☑ Arrange for professional development support.
- ☑ Implement teacher technology committees.

Phase One

- Identify the decision makers (e.g., administration, committees, school board).

- Gather information about the current state of technology in your school or district.

- Develop a vision for technology and align to the CCSS.

- Plan a sequence of professional development that is differentiated to meet the needs of the teachers.

Phase Two

- Provide continued support for technology implementation through professional learning communities (PLCs) and leadership teams.

- Include a variety of areas of expertise (e.g., special education, administration, ELL instruction).

TOOL #38: SCHOOL LITERACY PLANNER

The CCSS were designed with literacy as a foundation for college and career readiness. Creating a schoolwide literacy plan establishes a common set of goals and expectations that leads to greater student success. Tool #38 (**page 117 and Figure 7.3**) will help you develop a literacy plan that places particular emphasis on text complexity and on argumentation writing skills. This tool is a visual representation of a planning process, rather than something to be filled out. Consider keeping it displayed in your meeting area as your team formulates a literacy plan. The following annotated example indicates factors that one school discussed in their first-year planning process. Bear in mind, it will vary considerably from school to school.

EXAMPLE TOOL #38: SCHOOL LITERACY PLANNER

Data Analysis

- What areas of reading, writing, and literacy are most difficult for our students?
- Based on their reading and writing scores, are students with special needs achieving at the highest levels for their disability?
- What are the opportunities for independent reading and writing?
- What supports for struggling students are present in our school, neighborhood, and community?

Prioritize and Set Goals

- Create a checklist of goals based on the data analysis and corresponding timeline.

Identify Instructional Strategies

- Identify *research-based* strategies and methods.
- Create a professional development plan to support the implementation of identified strategies and methods.

Identify Indicators to Monitor Results

- Select data resources that include teacher-based assessments and district assessments to monitor results.

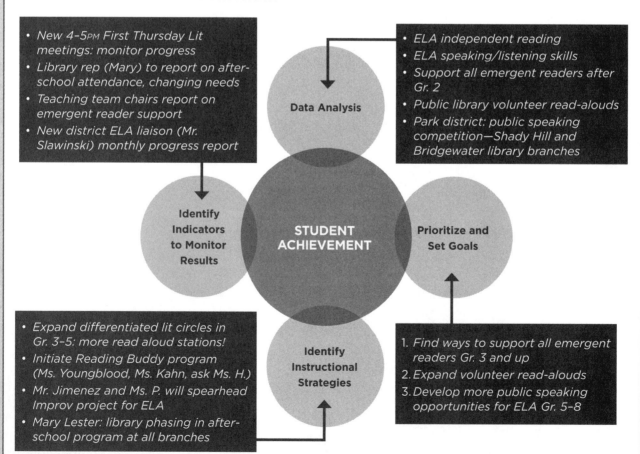

- *New 4–5PM First Thursday Lit meetings: monitor progress*
- *Library rep (Mary) to report on after-school attendance, changing needs*
- *Teaching team chairs report on emergent reader support*
- *New district ELA liaison (Mr. Slawinski) monthly progress report*

- *ELA independent reading*
- *ELA speaking/listening skills*
- *Support all emergent readers after Gr. 2*
- *Public library volunteer read-alouds*
- *Park district: public speaking competition—Shady Hill and Bridgewater library branches*

Data Analysis

Identify Indicators to Monitor Results

STUDENT ACHIEVEMENT

Prioritize and Set Goals

Identify Instructional Strategies

- *Expand differentiated lit circles in Gr. 3–5: more read aloud stations!*
- *Initiate Reading Buddy program (Ms. Youngblood, Ms. Kahn, ask Ms. H.)*
- *Mr. Jimenez and Ms. P. will spearhead Improv project for ELA*
- *Mary Lester: library phasing in after-school program at all branches*

1. *Find ways to support all emergent readers Gr. 3 and up*
2. *Expand volunteer read-alouds*
3. *Develop more public speaking opportunities for ELA Gr. 5–8*

Data Analysis

- What areas of reading, writing, and literacy are most difficult for our students?
- Based on their reading and writing scores, are students with special needs achieving at the highest levels for their disability?
- What are the opportunities for independent reading and writing?
- What supports for struggling students are present in our school, neighborhood, and community?

Prioritize and Set Goals

- Create a checklist of goals based on the data analysis and corresponding timeline.

Identify Instructional Strategies

- Identify *research-based* strategies and methods.
- Create a professional development plan to support the implementation of identified strategies and methods.

Identify Indicators to Monitor Results

- Select data resources that include teacher-based assessments and district assessments to monitor results.

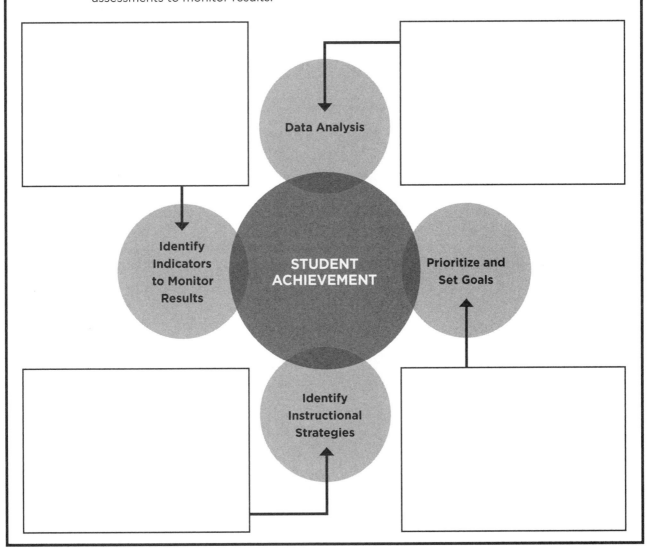

TOOL #39: FORMATIVE ASSESSMENT PLANNER

Formative assessment is, of course, nothing new. An effective formative assessment plan includes regular checks for understanding and for student projects that demonstrate mastery of skills and content knowledge. Formative assessment is central to the kind of responsive teaching that leads to the skill development articulated in the Common Core. The formative assessment planner presented in Tool #39 (**pages 120–122**) will help you develop a comprehensive plan that is aligned to the CCSS. The graphic in **Figure 7.4** and accompanying text provides an overview for creating and implementing a formative assessment plan.

SIX STEPS TO CREATING A FORMATIVE ASSESSMENT PLAN

Step 6: Monitor
Use classroom performance assessment tools and formative assessments to continuously monitor student progress toward the goals.

Step 1: Identify
Perform a close reading of the CCSS document to identify the standards for student success during the school year.

Step 2: Analyze and Align
Analyze existing assessment data, and then align curriculum and desired instruction results.

Step 5: Select Strategies
Select teaching strategies that will align with the focused curriculum (from Step 4), while developing the content knowledge and skills specified in the standards (from Step 3).

Step 3: Modify
Use professional judgment to make modifications to standards (from Step 1) as a result of data analysis (from Step 2).

Step 4: Focus
Focus curriculum and instruction on the big ideas and the essential questions.

Formative Assessment Types

The chart below provides ideas for formative assessments.
Indicate in which units you will use each type of assessment.

Sample Categories of Formative Assessment	Types of Formative Assessment	Instructional Unit in Which This Assessment Will Be Integrated
Observations	**Anecdotal notes** (Teacher makes short observational notes during lessons and classroom activities.)	
	Anecdotal notebook (Teacher keeps a notebook of general or individual observations of students during instructional activities.)	
	Anecdotal notecards (Teacher creates a card file of student observations.)	
	Sticky notes (Teacher takes notes during instruction and attaches them in a journal for reference.)	
Questions	**Well-framed questions** (Teacher focuses questions on high-order thinking skills rather than factual knowledge.)	
	Think time (Teacher allows students time to just think on a topic, or even jot down some of their ideas.)	
	Wait time (Teacher allows about five seconds after asking a question to let students come up with their responses.)	
Graphic Organizers	**Visual word association** (Teacher says a vocabulary word and students draw a picture or example of the word.)	
	Mind maps (Students use drawings or photos to portray a specific idea, word, or concept.)	
	Verbal word association (Teacher says a vocabulary word and students write a list of synonyms.)	
Logs	**Response logs** (Students write their reactions to a lesson, a book, etc.)	
	Learning logs (Students record the process they went through when learning something new.)	

CONTINUED ON NEXT PAGE

Sample Categories of Formative Assessment	Types of Formative Assessment	Instructional Unit in Which This Assessment Will Be Integrated
Discussion	**Create a discussion** (Teacher uses open-ended questions to develop students' critical thinking.)	
	Decision-making chart (Students write reasons for their opinion and reasons against their opinion.)	
	In-class debates (Teacher divides the classroom into two groups, giving them different sides of an argument.)	
Slips	**Exit slips** (Students fill out slips at the end of a lesson responding to a question the teacher asks.)	
	Admit slips (Students fill out slips before class responding to questions regarding the previous night's homework or the previous day's lesson.)	
Student Assessments	**Peer assessments** (Students form groups and share and check the quality of each other's work.)	
	Self-assessments (Students review their own work, mark mistakes, and also record their strengths and weaknesses.)	
Presentations	**Practice presentations** (Students have a day or two to practice their presentations; the teacher can watch and compare to the final presentation.)	
	T-Chart (On one side list all the positive qualities of the presentation, on the other all the negative qualities.)	
	Peer review (Students closely watch the presentations, writing down what was confusing or helpful about their peer's presentation.)	

CONTINUED ON NEXT PAGE

Sample Categories of Formative Assessment	Types of Formative Assessment	Instructional Unit in Which This Assessment Will Be Integrated
Kinesthetic Assessments	**Debate circles** (Students sit in two circles of equal number, one inside the other; the inner circle faces outward and the outer circle faces inward. An opinion question is asked. Students explain their beliefs to the person facing them from the other circle.)	
	Inside-outside circles (Students stand in two circles of equal number, one inside the other; the inner circle faces outward and the outer circle faces inward. Students discuss a book or answer questions with the person facing them.)	
	Math graphing (Teacher forms a graph plane on the floor with available materials and tells students to walk to specific coordinates.)	
Whiteboards	**Individual/group slates** (Students answer problems on their own boards, and then hold them up for the teacher to check.)	
Groups	**Interest groups** (Students divide into groups based on common interests, such as whether they prefer red or blue.)	
	Four corners (Each corner of the room is given a position: strongly agree, agree, disagree, and strongly disagree. After a statement is read, students choose a corner, and the class discusses their points of view.)	
Group Discussions	**Think-pair-share** (Students answer a question on their own, and then pair up to discuss their findings. Finally, the class shares their findings.)	
	Think-pair-square-share (Similar to think-pair-share, students answer a question on their own, and then pair up to discuss their findings. But here, they join with another pair and talk further before sharing with the class.)	
	Appointment clock (Students choose three peers and meet with each for 15 minutes.)	

TOOL #40: MASTER ASSESSMENT SCHEDULE

Assessment is an integral part of curriculum and instruction. Creating a plan that implements a wide variety of assessment strategies is an effective means to comprehensively address the development of student skills and content knowledge. A master assessment schedule also creates greater opportunities for teachers to reflect on instruction and plan adjustments accordingly. Not all assessments should be standardized tests. Provide students with opportunities to develop projects, portfolios, or technology-based documents that demonstrate content knowledge and developed skills. Tool #40 (**page 125 and Figure 7.5**) will help you develop a master assessment schedule that includes a variety of assessments for students to demonstrate what they know and understand.

EXAMPLE TOOL #40: MASTER ASSESSMENT SCHEDULE

Formative Assessments (Classroom-based)	Weeks 1–5	Weeks 6–10	Weeks 11–15	Weeks 16–20	Weeks 21–25	Weeks 26–30	Weeks 31–35	Weeks 36–40
Sticky notes	✔							
Framing questions		✔			✔		✔	
Mind maps			✔					
Vocabulary graphic organizers	✔			✔		✔		✔
Learning logs			✔		✔		✔	
Kinesthetic activities	✔	✔		✔				

Select formative assessments to list and determine when to focus on them during the school year.

Formative Assessments (Classroom-based)	Weeks 1-5	Weeks 6-10	Weeks 11-15	Weeks 16-20	Weeks 21-25	Weeks 26-30	Weeks 31-35	Weeks 36-40

Summative Assessments	Weeks 1-5	Weeks 6-10	Weeks 11-15	Weeks 16-20	Weeks 21-25	Weeks 26-30	Weeks 31-35	Weeks 36-40
School-Based Assessment								
District-Level Assessment								
CCSS National Assessment (PARCC or Smarter Balanced)								

Closing Thoughts and Advice

As I write this final chapter, decisions regarding the CCSS are still being made. Some states are still debating whether or not the adoption makes sense for their population. And the assessment consortia: PARCC (the Partnership for Assessment of Readiness for College and Careers) and Smarter Balanced are still drafting and revising the new assessments. All of this would be stressful under the best of circumstances. It's potentially overwhelming for those teachers who find their own professional evaluations are tied to their student assessment results. Here are some last bits of wisdom and advice to help support you during this transition:

1. **Remind yourself that you can't do it all at once.** Choose three to five areas that you will focus on for the next school year. It could be text complexity, argumentation and writing, helping students develop claims in mathematics, and integrating more technology. It doesn't matter which areas you pick. But choose just three—certainly no more than five—and do your very best to focus on those identified areas.

2. **Gather resources and ideas from your teacher colleagues in all content areas.** A hallmark feature of the Common Core State Standards is that students will now be expected to read a wide variety of complex and challenging texts in a variety of contexts, so brainstorm with colleagues to explore ways to meet this rigorous expectation. In making this one of your focus areas, you'll find that it also helps you meet many of the other skills that are articulated in the CCSS.

3. **Work with your administration to develop a strong literacy plan** within your school and district. This literacy plan, which includes reading and writing, should reflect a vision that will guide teachers as they make important decisions about teaching skills and content.

4. **Focus on curriculum structures such as Understanding by Design, inquiry learning, project-based learning, mastery learning, and differentiated instruction.** All of these structures provide a curriculum framework that encourages students to ask questions and seek answers through a wide variety of sources and applications. This is the meat of the CCSS. It's not about what you know; it's about *how you use* what you know.

5. **Effective teaching and learning will always result in a solid performance in the national assessments.** This is the response I give to teachers and administrators who ask me, "How do you prepare your students for the new assessments?" Data gleaned from many studies supports this assertion. When students are able to think critically and apply their skills, they are prepared for any situation that requires them to demonstrate what they know and understand.

6. **Teachers need time to collaborate, plan, and write curriculum that meets these new standards and expectations.** I cannot stress enough how important this is. As the CCSS document explains, you know best how students in a given context can develop the skills and content knowledge articulated in the new standards. But you need time to produce the appropriate curriculum and necessary classroom materials. Only then will students have learning experiences that promote the development of college and career readiness skills.

7. **Don't throw out your current curriculum!** Instead, use the CCSS as a lens to audit, reflect upon, and revise your curriculum to meet the new expectations.

8. **We need to go back to what we all first knew as teachers.** That joy we find in creating exciting teaching and learning experiences for our students is what drew us to the profession in the first place. This kind of teaching is not found in test-driven education. We are now embarking on a corpus of standards that are meant to be generative models and frameworks for skills and content knowledge. To ensure fidelity to the Common Core State Standards, educators must be the caretakers of learning experiences that engage and challenge students to prepare for college and careers.

9. **Take the time with your colleagues to closely read the entire CCSS document.** Do not take shortcuts. The introduction and appendices, in particular, are packed with important information that will give you grounding for this new paradigm. The tools that are featured in this book are designed to guide you from the fundamentals of the Common Core State Standards document to actual curriculum implementation.

10. **Try to embrace this shift to the new standards,** because the CCSS document places great value on teachers. The CCSS authors recognize the teacher's ability to provide students with the learning experiences they need to be college and career ready. Like many of my teacher colleagues, I am often leery of new initiatives. Yet, in spite of my misgivings, I was relieved to identify the research, wisdom, and respect for educators that embody the Common Core State Standards. Once you have progressed through all of the tools in this book, you'll be well prepared for the Common Core era.

Finally, I would be remiss in suggesting that the Common Core State Standards are a panacea for all of the challenges that we face in education today. They aren't perfect and it would be challenging to create a "perfect" set of standards. Our classrooms are far too complex. I do, however, see the CCSS document as a means for educators to assert their professional expertise. In my view, there is nothing more important than our work as educators as we prepare our students for successful futures.

References and Resources

REFERENCES

Anderson, L. W., D. R. Krathwohl, and B. S. Bloom. *A Taxonomy for Learning, Teaching, and Assessing: A Revision of Bloom's Taxonomy of Educational Objectives (Complete ed.)*. New York: Longman, 2001.

Appleman, D. *Adolescent Literacy and the Teaching of Reading: Lessons for Teachers of Literature*. Urbana, IL: National Council of Teachers of English, 2010.

Beck, I. L., M. G. McKeown, and L. Kucan. *Bringing Words to Life: Robust Vocabulary Instruction*. New York: Guilford Press, 2002.

Beers, G. K. *When Kids Can't Read, What Teachers Can Do: A Guide for Teachers, 6–12*. Portsmouth, NH: Heinemann, 2003.

Blachowicz, C. L., and P. Fisher. *Teaching Vocabulary in All Classrooms*. Upper Saddle River, NJ: Merrill/Prentice Hall, 2005.

Carver, R. P. *The Causes of High and Low Reading Achievement*. Mahwah, NJ: Lawrence Erlbaum Associates, 2000.

Chall, Jeanne. *The Academic Achievement Challenge*. New York: Guilford Publications, Inc., 2000.

Gardner, H. *Intelligence Reframed: Multiple Intelligences for the 21st Century*. New York: Basic Books, 1999.

Graff, G., and C. Birkenstein. *They Say, I Say: The Moves That Matter in Academic Writing*. New York: W.W. Norton & Co., 2010.

Heller, R., and C. L. Greenleaf. *Literacy Instruction in the Content Areas: Getting to the Core of Middle and High School Improvement*. Washington, DC: Alliance for Excellent Education, 2007.

Hillocks, G. *Teaching Argument Writing, Grades 6–12: Supporting Claims with Relevant Evidence and Clear Reasoning*. Portsmouth, NH: Heinemann, 2011.

International Reading Association. *Making a Difference Means Making It Different: Honoring Children's Rights to Excellent Reading Instruction*. Newark, DE: International Reading Association, 2000.

Marzano, R. J., D. Pickering, and J. E. Pollock. *Classroom Instruction that Works: Research-Based Strategies for Increasing Student Achievement*. Alexandria, VA: ASCD, 2001.

Montgomery, J. "Vocabulary Interventions for RTI: Tiers 1, 2, 3." Paper presented at the Annual Convention of the American Speech-Language-Hearing Association, Boston, MA, November 2007.

Montgomery, K. *MAVA-Montgomery Assessment of Vocabulary Acquisition.* Greenville, SC: Super Duper Publications, Inc., 2008.

National Governors Association Center for Best Practices, Council of Chief State School Officers. *Common Core State Standards.* Washington, DC: National Governors Association Center for Best Practices, Council of Chief State School Officers, 2010.

Tomlinson, C. A. *The Differentiated Classroom: Responding to the Needs of All Learners.* Alexandria, VA: ASCD, 1999.

Tomlinson, C. A. *Fulfilling the Promise of the Differentiated Classroom.* Alexandria, VA: ASCD, 2003.

Tomlinson, C. A. *How to Differentiate Instruction in Mixed Ability Classrooms.* Alexandria, VA: ASCD, 2001.

Wiggins, G. P., and J. McTighe. *Understanding by Design.* Boston: Pearson, 2005.

RESOURCES

Print Resources

Allyn, P. *Be Core Ready: Powerful, Effective Steps to Implementing and Achieving the Common Core State Standards.* Boston: Pearson, 2013. This transformational book addresses curriculum, close reading, text complexity, and care practices for ELL and special needs students.

Baska, J. *Using the Common Core State Standards for English Language Arts with Gifted and Advanced Learners.* Waco, TX: Prufrock Press, 2013. This book provides teachers and administrators with examples and strategies to implement the new Common Core State Standards (CCSS) for advanced learners at all stages of development in K–12 schools.

Beers, G. K., and E. R. Probst. *Notice and Note: Strategies for Close Reading.* Portsmouth, NH: Heinemann, 2013. This book introduces six signposts that alert readers to significant moments in a work of literature and encourage students to read closely.

Calkins, L., M. Ehrenworth, and C. Lehman. *Pathways to the Common Core: Accelerating Achievement.* Portsmouth, NH: Heinemannn, 2012. This book helps teachers, school leaders, and professional learning communities navigate the gap between their current literacy practices and the ideals of the Common Core.

Core, I. *Common Core Curriculum Maps in English Language Arts, Grades K–5.* San Francisco: Jossey-Bass, 2012. The research-based curriculum maps in this book present a comprehensive, coherent sequence of thematic units for teaching the skills outlined in the CCSS for English language arts in grades K–5.

Core, I. *Common Core Curriculum Maps in English Language Arts, Grades 6–8.* San Francisco: Jossey-Bass, 2012. The research-based curriculum maps in this book present a comprehensive, coherent sequence of thematic units for teaching the skills outlined in the CCSS for English language arts in grades 6–8.

Crawford, J. *Aligning Your Curriculum to the Common Core State Standards*. Thousand Oaks, CA: Corwin Press, 2012. This hands-on guide takes you through a proven process for implementing the new Common Core State Standards and includes access to Internet-based software for curriculum mapping.

Diller, D. *Math Work Stations: Independent Learning You Can Count On, K–2*. Portland, ME: Stenhouse Publishers, 2011. *Math Work Stations* includes ideas to help children develop conceptual understanding and skills, use math vocabulary to talk about mathematical thinking, and connect big ideas to meaningful independent exploration and practice. This book details how to set up, manage, and keep math stations going throughout the year.

Drake, S. M. *Creating Standards-Based Integrated Curriculum: The Common Core State Standards Edition*. Thousand Oaks, CA: Corwin, 2012. This updated edition serves as a roadmap through the CCSS, with clear guidance on multidisciplinary, interdisciplinary, and transdisciplinary approaches to creating an integrated curriculum.

Fisher, D., N. Frey, and D. Lapp. *Teaching Students to Read Like Detectives: Comprehending, Analyzing, and Discussing Text*. Bloomington, IN: Solution Tree Press, 2012.

In this comprehensive guide, the authors explore the relationship between text, learner, and learning through discussion and rhetorical writing at the elementary, middle, and high school levels.

Hawkins, R., and R. J. Manley. *Making the Common Core Standards Work: Using Professional Development to Build World-Class Schools*. Thousand Oaks, CA.: Corwin, 2013. Written for school leaders, this practical guide provides a blueprint for implementing and exceeding the Common Core State Standards, with a focus on empowering teachers and staff.

Heard, G. *Poetry Lessons to Meet the Common Core State Standards: Exemplar Poems with Engaging Lessons and Response Activities That Help Students Read, Understand, and Appreciate Poetry*. New York: Scholastic Teaching Resources, 2013. This book guides students to identify figurative language; to hear rhyme, rhythm, and other poetic conventions; and to explore imagery and theme—and then determine how these elements deepen their understanding of the poem. Students gain a thorough knowledge of poetic elements, which helps them meet Common Core State Standards in literature and language.

Hull, T. H., R. H. Miles, and D. S. Balka. *The Common Core Mathematics Standards: Transforming Practice Through Team Leadership*. Thousand Oaks, CA: Corwin Press, 2012. This professional development resource includes techniques and reproducible tools to help principals and math leaders drive the change process for implementing the CCSS in math.

Kendall, J. S. *Understanding Common Core State Standards*. Alexandria, VA: ASCD, 2011. This book explains the Common Core standards and offers ideas for strengthening teaching and learning across the United States, and what you can do to make the most of this opportunity for change.

Neuman, S. B., and L. B. Gambrell. *Quality Reading Instruction in the Age of Common Core Standards.* Newark, DE: International Reading Association, 2013.

This book covers key areas of the CCSS—such as information texts, text complexity, and vocabulary development—and makes the most of twenty-first-century tools and technology.

Owocki, G. *The Common Core Lesson Book, K–5: Working with Increasingly Complex Literature, Informational Text, and Foundational Reading Skills.* Portsmouth, NH: Heinemann, 2012. *The Common Core Lesson Book* empowers teachers with a comprehensive framework for implementation that enhances existing curriculum and extends it to meet Common Core goals.

Peery, A. B., and M. D. Wiggs. *Navigating the English Language Arts Common Core State Standards.* Englewood, CO: Lead + Learn Press, 2012. This handbook helps teachers and administrators sort through the English language arts standards and focus on the key components of the CCSS. This is the second of a four-book series that started with *Navigating Implementation of the Common Core State Standards.*

Reeves, D. B., and M. D. Wiggs. *Navigating Implementation of the Common Core State Standards*, Getting Ready for the Common Core Handbook Series. Englewood, CO: Lead + Learn Press, 2012. The first in a series of four, this book provides background on the CCSS and helps create a plan to implement the standards.

Ryan, S., D. Frazee, and J. Kendall. *Common Core Standards for High School English Language Arts: A Quick-Start Guide.* Alexandria, VA: ASCD, 2012. This book explains the structure, terminology, and emphases of the Common Core standards for English language arts and literacy at the high school level.

Santoyo, P., and B. M. Peiser. *Leverage Leadership: A Practical Guide to Building Exceptional Schools.* San Francisco: Jossey-Bass, 2012. This book demonstrates how leaders can raise their schools to greatness by following a core set of principles. These seven principles, or "levers," allow for consistent, transformational, and replicable growth.

Santoyo, P., A. Settles, and J. Worrell. *Great Habits, Great Readers: A Practical Guide for K–4 Reading in the Light of Common Core.* San Francisco: Wiley & Sons, Inc., 2013. This book includes the strategies, systems, and lessons from the top classrooms that bring the habits of reading to life, creating countless quality opportunities for students to take one of the most complex skills we as people can know and to perform it fluently and easily.

Silver, H. F., and R. T. Dewing. *The Core Six Essential Strategies for Achieving Excellence with the Common Core.* Alexandria: ASCD, 2012. This book provides strategies that help with the six categories: reading for meaning, comparing and contrasting, inductive learning, circle of knowledge, writing to learn, and vocabulary's code.

Young, S. *English Language Arts Station Activities: For Common Core State Standards.* Portland, ME: Walch Education, 2011. This book includes a collection of station-based activities to provide students with opportunities to practice and apply the skills and concepts they learn in class.

Online Resources

Achieve the Core

www.achievethecore.org

This website contains many resources, from learning how to unpack the standards to useful tools and rubrics for implementation.

ASCD Common Core State Standards Resource Site

www.ascd.org/common-core-state-standards/common-core.aspx

ASCD is an endorsing partner of the Common Core initiative and provides the resources necessary to gain an accurate understanding of the Common Core initiative.

Common Core State Standards

www.corestandards.org

This website provides clear standards for what students are expected to learn, and allows teachers and parents to know what they need to do to help them learn.

Common Core State Standards: Where Does Differentiation Fit?

www.ascd.org/professional-development/webinars/tomlinson-and-britt-webinar.aspx

This website contains PDFs and webinars that focus on using various methodologies of teaching to help different styles of learners.

Creating Text Sets

www.learner.org/workshops/tml/workshop4/teaching.html

This website contains numerous workshops that allow students to get involved in different learning techniques.

Edutopia

www.edutopia.org/common-core-state-standards-resources

Edutopia provides a guide that helps make sense of the Common Core State Standards initiative and that allows people to join the conversation about the new CCSS concepts.

Mathematics Common Core State Standards Toolbox

www.ccsstoolbox.com

This website is designed to support districts working to meet the challenge and the opportunity of the new standards by providing tools and instructional materials that help teachers better understand and implement the Common Core State Standards for Mathematics, or CCSSM.

National Association for Elementary School Principals

www.naesp.org/common-core-state-standards-resources

The NAESP website contains specific resources—including books, articles, and webinars—that relate to the Common Core State Standards.

Partnership for Assessment of Readiness for College and Careers Assessment Consortium

www.parcconline.org

PARCC is a multistate consortium that is developing next-generation K–12 assessments in English and math. The consortium works to keep students on track and to help educators guide learning and instruction.

Read Write Think

www.readwritethink.org

This website provides a variety of resources for classrooms, as well as for parent and for after-school programs. Resources include books, fun activities, and lesson plans that inspire young students.

Smarter Balanced Assessment Consortium

www.smarterbalanced.org

Smarter Balanced is a state-led consortium developing assessments aligned to the Common Core State Standards in English language arts/literacy and in mathematics that are designed to help prepare all students graduate from high school and be ready for college or a career.

Student-Centered Learning

www.studentsatthecenter.org

This website provides numerous articles that focus on issues involving learning as well as teaching.

Teaching Channel

www.teachingchannel.org

Teaching Channel is a video showcase—on the Internet and on TV—of innovative and effective teaching practices in U.S. schools.

Appendix: Tool #18
The CCSS ELA Grades 3–8 Matrices

In the following section, I have included the graphic organizer from Tool #18 for six core grade levels in English language arts. Feel free to fill in or duplicate these pages for use in PLCs and curriculum planning groups. **Please note: These are only a sampling of available matrices.** A full set of customizable standards matrices (over 300 pages) is included in the digital download for all grade levels and subject areas. See page ix for instructions on how to access the digital content.

GRADE 3 ENGLISH LANGUAGE ARTS COMMON CORE STATE STANDARDS

Unpack CCSS and articulate from a student point of view. Use school data and teacher observation to add details and information regarding each standard.

CCSS	Converted/Unpacked Standard	Observations from Analysis	When in the year will this standard be covered?
Reading for Literature			
CC.3.R.L.1 Key Ideas and Details: Ask and answer questions to demonstrate understanding of a text, referring explicitly to the text as the basis for the answers.	*Example: I can ask questions about the text, and read to find answers.* *I can answer questions about the text.*		
CC.3.R.L.2 Key Ideas and Details: Recount stories, including fables, folktales, and myths from diverse cultures; determine the central message, lesson, or moral and explain how it is conveyed through key details in the text.			
CC.3.R.L.3 Key Ideas and Details: Describe characters in a story (e.g., their traits, motivations, or feelings) and explain how their actions contribute to the sequence of events.			
CC.3.R.L.4 Craft and Structure: Determine the meaning of words and phrases as they are used in a text, distinguishing literal from nonliteral language.			
CC.3.R.L.5 Craft and Structure: Refer to parts of stories, dramas, and poems when writing or speaking about a text, using terms such as chapter, scene, and stanza; describe how each successive part builds on earlier sections.			
CC.3.R.L.6 Craft and Structure: Distinguish their own point of view from that of the narrator or those of the characters.			

From *Common Core State Standards for English Language Arts & Literacy in History/Social Studies, Science, and Technical Subjects.*
Copyright © 2010. National Governors Association Center for Best Practices and Council of Chief State School Officers. All rights reserved.

GRADE 3 ENGLISH LANGUAGE ARTS COMMON CORE STATE STANDARDS

Unpack CCSS and articulate from a student point of view. Use school data and teacher observation to add details and information regarding each.

CCSS	Converted/Unpacked Standard	Observations from Analysis	When in the year will this standard be covered?
CC.3.R.L.7 Integration of Knowledge and Ideas: Explain how specific aspects of a text's illustrations contribute to what is conveyed by the words in a story (e.g., create mood, emphasize aspects of a character or setting).			
CC.3.R.L.9 Integration of Knowledge and Ideas: Compare and contrast the themes, settings, and plots of stories written by the same author about the same or similar characters (e.g., in books from a series).			
CC.3.R.L.10 Range of Reading and Complexity of Text: By the end of the year, read and comprehend literature, including stories, dramas, and poetry, at the high end of the grades 2–3 text complexity band independently and proficiently.			
Reading for Informational Text			
CC.3.R.I.1 Key Ideas and Details: Ask and answer questions to demonstrate understanding of a text, referring explicitly to the text as the basis for the answers.	*Example: I can ask and answer questions about the text.* *I can talk about what the text means when answering questions.*		
CC.3.R.I.2 Key Ideas and Details: Determine the main idea of a text; recount the key details and explain how they support the main idea.			

APPENDIX: TOOL #18: THE CCSS ELA GRADES 3–8 MATRICES (FOR ALL OTHER GRADES/SUBJECTS, SEE THE DIGITAL DOWNLOAD.)

GRADE 3 ENGLISH LANGUAGE ARTS COMMON CORE STATE STANDARDS

Unpack CCSS and articulate from a student point of view. Use school data and teacher observation to add details and information regarding each standard.

CCSS	Converted/Unpacked Standard	Observations from Analysis	When in the year will this standard be covered?
CC.3.R.I.3 Key Ideas and Details: Describe the relationship between a series of historical events, scientific ideas or concepts, or steps in technical procedures in a text, using language that pertains to time, sequence, and cause/effect.			
CC.3.R.I.4 Craft and Structure: Determine the meaning of general academic and domain-specific words and phrases in a text relevant to a *grade 3 topic or subject area.*			
CC.3.R.I.5 Craft and Structure: Use text features and search tools (e.g., key words, sidebars, hyperlinks) to locate information relevant to a given topic efficiently.			
CC.3.R.I.6 Craft and Structure: Distinguish their own point of view from that of the author of a text.			
CC.3.R.I.7 Integration of Knowledge and Ideas: Use information gained from illustrations (e.g., maps, photographs) and the words in a text to demonstrate understanding of the text (e.g., where, when, why, and how key events occur).			
CC.3.R.I.8 Integration of Knowledge and Ideas: Describe the logical connection between particular sentences and paragraphs in a text (e.g., comparison, cause/effect, first/second/third in a sequence).			

GRADE 3 ENGLISH LANGUAGE ARTS COMMON CORE STATE STANDARDS

Unpack CCSS and articulate from a student point of view. Use school data and teacher observation to add details and information regarding each standard.

CCSS	Converted/Unpacked Standard	Observations from Analysis	When in the year will this standard be covered?
CC.3.R.I.9 Integration of Knowledge and Ideas: Compare and contrast the most important points and key details presented in two texts on the same topic.			
CC.3.R.I.10 Range of Reading and Level of Text Complexity: By the end of the year, read and comprehend informational texts, including history/social studies, science, and technical texts, at the high end of the grades 2–3 text complexity band independently and proficiently.			
Reading for Foundational Skills			
CC.3.R.F.3 Phonics and Word Recognition: Know and apply grade-level phonics and word analysis skills in decoding words.			
CC.3.R.F.3.a Phonics and Word Recognition: Identify and know the meaning of the most common prefixes and derivational suffixes.	*Example: I know the meaning of common prefixes and suffixes.*		
CC.3.R.F.3.b Phonics and Word Recognition: Decode words with common Latin suffixes.			
CC.3.R.F.3.c Phonics and Word Recognition: Decode multisyllable words.	*I can read multisyllable words.*		
CC.3.R.F.3.d Phonics and Word Recognition: Read grade-appropriate irregularly spelled words.			

APPENDIX: TOOL #18: THE CCSS ELA GRADES 3–8 MATRICES (FOR ALL OTHER GRADES/SUBJECTS, SEE THE DIGITAL DOWNLOAD.)

GRADE 3 ENGLISH LANGUAGE ARTS COMMON CORE STATE STANDARDS

Unpack CCSS and articulate from a student point of view. ation regarding each standard.

CCSS	Converted/Unpacked Standard	Observations from Analysis	When in the year will this standard be covered?
CC.3.R.F.4 Fluency: Read with sufficient accuracy and fluency to support comprehension.			
CC.3.R.F.4.a Fluency: Read on-level text with purpose and understanding.			
CC.3.R.F.4.b Fluency: Read on-level prose and poetry orally with accuracy, appropriate rate, and expression on successive readings.			
CC.3.R.F.4.c Fluency: Use context to confirm or self-correct word recognition and understanding, rereading as necessary.			
Writing Standards			
CC.3.W.1 Text Types and Purposes: Write opinion pieces on familiar topics or texts, supporting a point of view with reasons.	*Example: I can write opinion pieces on topics and texts.* *I can support my POV in writing.*		
CC.3.W.1.a Text Types and Purposes: Introduce the topic or text they are writing about, state an opinion, and create an organizational structure that lists reasons.			

GRADE 3 ENGLISH LANGUAGE ARTS COMMON CORE STATE STANDARDS

Unpack CCSS and articulate from a student point of view. Use school data and teacher observation to add details and information regarding each standard.

CCSS	Converted/Unpacked Standard	Observations from Analysis	When in the year will this standard be covered?
CC.3.W.1.b Text Types and Purposes: Provide reasons that support the opinion.			
CC.3.W.1.c Text Types and Purposes: Use linking words and phrases (e.g., *because, therefore, since, for example*) to connect opinion and reasons.			
CC.3.W.1.d Text Types and Purposes: Provide a concluding statement or section.			
CC.3.W.2 Text Types and Purposes: Write informative/explanatory texts to examine a topic and convey ideas and information clearly.			
CC.3.W.2.a Text Types and Purposes: Introduce a topic and group related information together; include illustrations when useful to aiding comprehension.			
CC.3.W.2.b Text Types and Purposes: Develop the topic with facts, definitions, and details.			

APPENDIX: TOOL #18: THE CCSS ELA GRADES 3–8 MATRICES (FOR ALL OTHER GRADES/SUBJECTS, SEE THE DIGITAL DOWNLOAD.)

GRADE 3 ENGLISH LANGUAGE ARTS COMMON CORE STATE STANDARDS

Unpack CCSS and articulate from a student point of view. Use school data and teacher observation to add details and information regarding each standard.

CCSS	Converted/Unpacked Standard	Observations from Analysis	When in the year will this standard be covered?
CC.3.W.2.c Text Types and Purposes: Use linking words and phrases (e.g., *also, another, and, more, but*) to connect ideas within categories of information.			
CC.3.W.2.d Text Types and Purposes: Provide a concluding statement or section.			
CC.3.W.3 Text Types and Purposes: Write narratives to develop real or imagined experiences or events using effective technique, descriptive details, and clear event sequences.			
CC.3.W.3.a Text Types and Purposes: Establish a situation and introduce a narrator and/or characters; organize an event sequence that unfolds naturally.			
CC.3.W.3.b Text Types and Purposes: Use dialogue and descriptions of actions, thoughts, and feelings to develop experiences and events or show the response of characters to situations.			
CC.3.W.3.c Text Types and Purposes: Use temporal words and phrases to signal event order.			

GRADE 3 ENGLISH LANGUAGE ARTS COMMON CORE STATE STANDARDS

Unpack CCSS and articulate from a student point of view. Use school data and teacher observation to add details and information regarding each standard.

CCSS	Converted/Unpacked Standard	Observations from Analysis	When in the year will this standard be covered?
CC.3.W.3.d Text Types and Purposes: Provide a sense of closure.			
CC.3.W.4 Production and Distribution of Writing: With guidance and support from adults, produce writing in which the development and organization are appropriate to task and purpose. (Grade-specific expectations for writing types are defined in standards 1–3 above.)			
CC.3.W.5 Production and Distribution of Writing: With guidance and support from peers and adults, develop and strengthen writing as needed by planning, revising, and editing. Editing for conventions should demonstrate command of Language standards 1–3 .			
CC.3.W.6 Production and Distribution of Writing: With guidance and support from adults, use technology to produce and publish writing (using keyboarding skills) as well as to interact and collaborate with others.			
CC.3.W.7 Research to Build and Present Knowledge: Conduct short research projects that build knowledge about a topic.			
CC.3.W.8 Research to Build and Present Knowledge: Recall information from experiences or gather information from print and digital sources; take brief notes on sources and sort evidence into provided categories.			

APPENDIX: TOOL #18: THE CCSS ELA GRADES 3–8 MATRICES (FOR ALL OTHER GRADES/SUBJECTS, SEE THE DIGITAL DOWNLOAD.)

GRADE 3 ENGLISH LANGUAGE ARTS COMMON CORE STATE STANDARDS

Unpack CCSS and articulate from a student point of view. Use school data and teacher observation to add details and information regarding each standard.

CCSS	Converted/Unpacked Standard	Observations from Analysis	When in the year will this standard be covered?
CC.3.W.10 Range of Writing: Write routinely over extended time frames (time for research, reflection, and revision) and shorter time frames (a single sitting or a day or two) for a range of discipline-specific tasks, purposes, and audiences.			
Speaking and Listening Standards			
CC.3.SL.1 Comprehension and Collaboration: Engage effectively in a range of collaborative discussions (one-on-one, in groups, and teacher-led) with diverse partners on *grade 3 topics and texts*, building on others' ideas and expressing their own clearly.	*Example: I can participate in one-on-one, group, and teacher-led discussions.* I can discuss my ideas, and build on other's ideas in a discussion.		
CC.3.SL.1.a Comprehension and Collaboration: Come to discussions prepared, having read or studied required material; explicitly draw on that preparation and other information known about the topic to explore ideas under discussion.			
CC.3.SL.1.b Comprehension and Collaboration: Follow agreed-upon rules for discussions (e.g., gaining the floor in respectful ways, listening to others with care, speaking one at a time about the topics and texts under discussion).			
CC.3.SL.1.c Comprehension and Collaboration: Ask questions to check understanding of information presented, stay on topic, and link their comments to the remarks of others.			

GRADE 3 ENGLISH LANGUAGE ARTS COMMON CORE STATE STANDARDS

Unpack CCSS and articulate from a student point of view. Use school data and teacher observation to add details and information regarding each standard.

CCSS	Converted/Unpacked Standard	Observations from Analysis	When in the year will this standard be covered?
CC.3.SL.1.d Comprehension and Collaboration: Explain their own ideas and understanding in light of the discussion.			
CC.3.SL.2 Comprehension and Collaboration: Determine the main ideas and supporting details of a text read aloud or information presented in diverse media and formats, including visually, quantitatively, and orally.			
CC.3.SL.3 Comprehension and Collaboration: Ask and answer questions about information from a speaker, offering appropriate elaboration and detail.			
CC.3.SL.4 Presentation of Knowledge and Ideas: Report on a topic or text, tell a story, or recount an experience with appropriate facts and relevant, descriptive details, speaking clearly at an understandable pace.			
CC.3.SL.5 Presentation of Knowledge and Ideas: Create engaging audio recordings of stories or poems that demonstrate fluid reading at an understandable pace; add visual displays when appropriate to emphasize or enhance certain facts or details.			
CC.3.SL.6 Presentation of Knowledge and Ideas: Speak in complete sentences when appropriate to task and situation in order to provide requested detail or clarification.			

APPENDIX: TOOL #18: THE CCSS ELA GRADES 3–8 MATRICES (FOR ALL OTHER GRADES/SUBJECTS, SEE THE DIGITAL DOWNLOAD.)

GRADE 3 ENGLISH LANGUAGE ARTS COMMON CORE STATE STANDARDS

Unpack CCSS and articulate from a student point of view. Use school data and teacher observation to add details and information regarding each standard.

CCSS	Converted/Unpacked Standard	Observations from Analysis	When in the year will this standard be covered?
CC.3.L1 Conventions of Standard English: Demonstrate command of the conventions of standard English grammar and usage when writing or speaking.			
CC.3.L.1.a Conventions of Standard English: Explain the function of nouns, pronouns, verbs, adjectives, and adverbs in general and their functions in particular sentences.	*Example: I can explain what nouns, pronouns, verbs, adjectives, and adverbs are, and how they are used in a sentence.*		
CC.3.L.1.b Conventions of Standard English: Form and use regular and irregular plural nouns.			
CC.3.L.1.c Conventions of Standard English: Use abstract nouns (e.g., *childhood*).			
CC.3.L.1.d Conventions of Standard English: Form and use regular and irregular verbs.			
CC.3.L.1.e Conventions of Standard English: Form and use the simple (e.g., *I walked; I walk; I will walk*) verb tenses.			
CC.3.L.1.f Conventions of Standard English: Ensure subject-verb and pronoun-antecedent agreement.			

GRADE 3 ENGLISH LANGUAGE ARTS COMMON CORE STATE STANDARDS

Unpack CCSS and articulate from a student point of view. Use school data and teacher observation to add details and information regarding each standard.

CCSS	Converted/Unpacked Standard	Observations from Analysis	When in the year will this standard be covered?
CC.3.L.1.g Conventions of Standard English: Form and use comparative and superlative adjectives and adverbs, and choose between them depending on what is to be modified.			
CC.3.L.1.h Conventions of Standard English: Use coordinating and subordinating conjunctions.			
CC.3.L.1.i Conventions of Standard English: Produce simple, compound, and complex sentences.			
CC.3.L.2 Conventions of Standard English: Demonstrate command of the conventions of standard English capitalization, punctuation, and spelling when writing.			
CC.3.L.2.a Conventions of Standard English: Capitalize appropriate words in titles.			
CC.3.L.2.b Conventions of Standard English: Use commas in addresses.			

APPENDIX: TOOL #18: THE CCSS ELA GRADES 3–8 MATRICES (FOR ALL OTHER GRADES/SUBJECTS, SEE THE DIGITAL DOWNLOAD.)

GRADE 3 ENGLISH LANGUAGE ARTS COMMON CORE STATE STANDARDS

Unpack CCSS and articulate from a student point of view. Use school data and teacher observation to add details and information regarding each standard.

CCSS	Converted/Unpacked Standard	Observations from Analysis	When in the year will this standard be covered?
CC.3.L.2.c Conventions of Standard English: Use commas and quotation marks in dialogue.			
CC.3.L.2.d Conventions of Standard English: Form and use possessives.			
CC.3.L.2.e Conventions of Standard English: Use conventional spelling for high-frequency and other studied words and for adding suffixes to base words (e.g., *sitting, smiled, cries, happiness*).			
CC.3.L.2.f Conventions of Standard English: Use spelling patterns and generalizations (e.g., word families, position-based spellings, syllable patterns, ending rules, meaningful word parts) in writing words.			
CC.3.L.2.g Conventions of Standard English: Consult reference materials, including beginning dictionaries, as needed to check and correct spellings.			
CC.3.L.3 Knowledge of Language: Use knowledge of language and its conventions when writing, speaking, reading, or listening.			

GRADE 3 ENGLISH LANGUAGE ARTS COMMON CORE STATE STANDARDS

Unpack CCSS and articulate from a student point of view. Use school data and teacher observation to add details and information regarding each standard.

CCSS	Converted/Unpacked Standard	Observations from Analysis	When in the year will this standard be covered?
CC.3.L.3.a Knowledge of Language: Choose words and phrases for effect.			
CC.3.L.3.b Knowledge of Language: Recognize and observe differences between the conventions of spoken and written standard English.			
CC.3.L.4 Vocabulary Acquisition and Use: Determine or clarify the meaning of unknown and multiple-meaning word and phrases based on *grade 3 reading and content,* choosing flexibly from a range of strategies.			
CC.3.L.4.a Vocabulary Acquisition and Use: Use sentence-level context as a clue to the meaning of a word or phrase.			
CC.3.L.4.b Vocabulary Acquisition and Use: Determine the meaning of the new word formed when a known affix is added to a known word (e.g., *agreeable/disagreeable, comfortable/uncomfortable, care/careless, heat/preheat*).			
CC.3.L.4.c Vocabulary Acquisition and Use: Use a known root word as a clue to the meaning of an unknown word with the same root (e.g., *company, companion*).			

APPENDIX: TOOL #18: THE CCSS ELA GRADES 3–8 MATRICES (FOR ALL OTHER GRADES/SUBJECTS, SEE THE DIGITAL DOWNLOAD.)

GRADE 3 ENGLISH LANGUAGE ARTS COMMON CORE STATE STANDARDS

Unpack CCSS and articulate from a student point of view. Use school data and teacher observation to add details and information regarding each standard.

CCSS	Converted/Unpacked Standard	Observations from Analysis	When in the year will this standard be covered?
CC.3.L.4.d Vocabulary Acquisition and Use: Use glossaries or beginning dictionaries, both print and digital, to determine or clarify the precise meaning of key words and phrases.			
CC.3.L.5 Vocabulary Acquisition and Use: Demonstrate understanding of word relationships and nuances in word meanings.			
CC.3.L.5.a Vocabulary Acquisition and Use: Distinguish the literal and nonliteral meanings of words and phrases in context (e.g., *take steps*).			
CC.3.L.5.b Vocabulary Acquisition and Use: Identify real-life connections between words and their use (e.g., describe people who are *friendly* or *helpful*).			
CC.3.L.5.c Vocabulary Acquisition and Use: Distinguish shades of meaning among related words that describe states of mind or degrees of certainty (e.g., *knew, believed, suspected, heard, wondered*).			
CC.3.L.6 Vocabulary Acquisition and Use: Acquire and use accurately grade-appropriate conversational, general academic, and domain-specific words and phrases, including those that signal spatial and temporal relationships (e.g., *After dinner that night we went looking for them*).			

GRADE 4 ENGLISH LANGUAGE ARTS CORE STATE STANDARDS

Unpack CCSS and articulate from a student point of view. Use school data and teacher observation to add details and information regarding each standard.

CCSS	Converted/Unpacked Standard	Observations from Analysis	When in the year will this standard be covered?
Reading for Literature			
CC.4.R.L.1 Key Ideas and Details: Refer to details and examples in a text when explaining what the text says explicitly and when drawing inferences from the text.	*Example: I can recall details and examples from the text.* *I can explain what the text says and means.*		
CC.4.R.L.2 Key Ideas and Details: Determine a theme of a story, drama, or poem from details in the text; summarize the text.			
CC.4.R.L.3 Key Ideas and Details: Describe in depth a character, setting, or event in a story or drama, drawing on specific details in the text (e.g., a character's thoughts, words, or actions).			
CC.4.R.L.4 Craft and Structure: Determine the meaning of words and phrases as they are used in a text, including those that allude to significant characters found in mythology (e.g., Herculean).			
CC.4.R.L.5 Craft and Structure: Explain major differences between poems, drama, and prose, and refer to the structural elements of poems (e.g., verse, rhythm, meter) and drama (e.g., casts of characters, setting descriptions, dialogue, stage directions) when writing or speaking about a text.			

APPENDIX: TOOL #18: THE CCSS ELA GRADES 3–8 MATRICES (FOR ALL OTHER GRADES/SUBJECTS, SEE THE DIGITAL DOWNLOAD.)

GRADE 4 ENGLISH LANGUAGE ARTS CORE STATE STANDARDS

Unpack CCSS and articulate from a student point of view. Use school data and teacher observation to add details and information regarding each standard.

CCSS	Converted/Unpacked Standard	Observations from Analysis	When in the year will this standard be covered?
CC.4.R.L.6 Craft and Structure: Compare and contrast the point of view from which different stories are narrated, including the difference between first- and third-person narrations.			
CC.4.R.L.7 Integration of Knowledge and Ideas: Make connections between the text of a story or drama and a visual or oral presentation of the text, identifying where each version reflects specific descriptions and directions in the text.			
CC.4.R.L.9 Integration of Knowledge and Ideas: Compare and contrast the treatment of similar themes and topics (e.g., opposition of good and evil) and patterns of events (e.g., the quest) in stories, myths, and traditional literature from different cultures.			
CC.4.R.L.10 Range of Reading and Complexity of Text: By the end of the year, read and comprehend literature, including stories, dramas, and poetry, in the grades 4–5 text complexity band proficiently, with scaffolding as needed at the high end of the range.			

GRADE 4 ENGLISH LANGUAGE ARTS CORE STATE STANDARDS

Unpack CCSS and articulate from a student point of view. Use school data and teacher observation to add details and information regarding each standard.

CCSS	Converted/Unpacked Standard	Observations from Analysis	When in the year will this standard be covered?
Reading for informational Text			
CC.4.R.I.1 Key Ideas and Details: Refer to details and examples in a text when explaining what the text says explicitly and when drawing inferences from the text.	*Example: I can recall details and examples from the text.* I can explain what the text says and means.		
CC.4.R.I.2 Key Ideas and Details: Determine the main idea of a text and explain how it is supported by key details; summarize the text.			
CC.4.R.I.3 Key Ideas and Details: Explain events, procedures, ideas, or concepts in a historical, scientific, or technical text, including what happened and why, based on specific information in the text.			
CC.4.R.I.4 Craft and Structure: Determine the meaning of general academic and domain-specific words or phrases in a text relevant to a *grade 4 topic or subject area.*			
CC.4.R.I.5 Craft and Structure: Describe the overall structure (e.g., chronology, comparison, cause/effect, problem/solution) of events, ideas, concepts, or information in a text or part of a text.			
CC.4.R.I.6 Craft and Structure: Compare and contrast a firsthand and secondhand account of the same event or topic; describe the differences in focus and the information provided.			

From Common Core State Standards for English Language Arts & Literacy in History/Social Studies, Science, and Technical Subjects.
Copyright © 2010. National Governors Association Center for Best Practices and Council of Chief State School Officers. All rights reserved.

APPENDIX: TOOL #18: THE CCSS ELA GRADES 3–8 MATRICES (FOR ALL OTHER GRADES/SUBJECTS, SEE THE DIGITAL DOWNLOAD.)

GRADE 4 ENGLISH LANGUAGE ARTS CORE STATE STANDARDS

Unpack CCSS and articulate from a student point of view Use school data and teacher observation to add details and information regarding each standard.

CCSS	Converted/Unpacked Standard	Observations from Analysis	When in the year will this standard be covered?
CC.4.R.I.7 Integration of Knowledge and Ideas: Interpret information presented visually, orally, or quantitatively (e.g., in charts, graphs, diagrams, time lines, animations, or interactive elements on Web pages) and explain how the information contributes to an understanding of the text in which it appears.			
CC.4.R.I.8 Integration of Knowledge and Ideas: Explain how an author uses reasons and evidence to support particular points in a text.			
CC.4.R.I.9 Integration of Knowledge and Ideas: Integrate information from two texts on the same topic in order to write or speak about the subject knowledgeably.			
CC.4.R.I.10 Range of Reading and Complexity of Text: By the end of year, read and comprehend informational texts, including history/social studies, science, and technical texts, in the grades 4–5 text complexity band proficiently, with scaffolding as necessary at the high end of the range.			

GRADE 4 ENGLISH LANGUAGE ARTS CORE STATE STANDARDS

Unpack CCSS and articulate from a student point of view. Use school data and teacher observation to add details and information regarding each standard.

CCSS	Converted/Unpacked Standard	Observations from Analysis	When in the year will this standard be covered?
Reading for Foundational Skills			
CC.4.R.F.3 Phonics and Word Recognition: Know and apply grade-level phonics and word analysis skills in decoding words.	*Example: I can read multisyllable words.*		
CC.4.R.F.3.a Phonics and Word Recognition: Use combined knowledge of all letter-sound correspondences, syllabication patterns, and morphology (e.g., roots and affixes) to read accurately unfamiliar multisyllabic words in context and out of context.			
CC.4.R.F.4 Fluency: Read with sufficient accuracy and fluency to support comprehension.			
CC.4.R.F.4.a Fluency: Read on-level text with purpose and understanding.			
CC.4.R.F.4.b Fluency: Read on-level prose and poetry orally with accuracy, appropriate rate, and expression on successive readings.			
CC.4.R.F.4.c Fluency: Use context to confirm or self-correct word recognition and understanding, rereading as necessary.			

APPENDIX: TOOL #18: THE CCSS ELA GRADES 3–8 MATRICES (FOR ALL OTHER GRADES/SUBJECTS, SEE THE DIGITAL DOWNLOAD.)

GRADE 4 ENGLISH LANGUAGE ARTS CORE STATE STANDARDS

Unpack CCSS and articulate from a student point of view. Use school data and teacher observation to add details and information regarding each standard.

CCSS	Converted/Unpacked Standard	Observations from Analysis	When in the year will this standard be covered?
Writing Standards			
CC.4.W.1 Text Types and Purposes: Write opinion pieces on topics or texts, supporting a point of view with reasons and information.	*Example: I can write my opinion and support it with reasons and information.*		
CC.4.W.1.a Text Types and Purposes: Introduce a topic or text clearly, state an opinion, and create an organizational structure in which related ideas are grouped to support the writer's purpose.			
CC.4.W.1.b Text Types and Purposes: Provide reasons that are supported by facts and details.			
CC.4.W.1.c Text Types and Purposes: Link opinion and reasons using words and phrases (e.g., *for instance, in order to, in addition*).			
CC.4.W.1.d Text Types and Purposes: Provide a concluding statement or section related to the opinion presented.			
CC.4.W.2 Text Types and Purposes: Write informative/explanatory texts to examine a topic and convey ideas and information clearly.			

GRADE 4 ENGLISH LANGUAGE ARTS CORE STATE STANDARDS

Unpack CCSS and articulate from a student point of view. Use school data and teacher observation to add details and information regarding each standard.

CCSS	Converted/Unpacked Standard	Observations from Analysis	When in the year will this standard be covered?
CC.4.W.2.a Text Types and Purposes: Introduce a topic clearly and group related information in paragraphs and sections; include formatting (e.g., headings), illustrations, and multimedia when useful to aiding comprehension.			
CC.4.W.2.b Text Types and Purposes: Develop the topic with facts, definitions, concrete details, quotations, or other information and examples related to the topic.			
CC.4.W.2.c Text Types and Purposes: Link ideas within categories of information using words and phrases (e.g., *another, for example, also, because*).			
CC.4.W.2.d Text Types and Purposes: Use precise language and domain-specific vocabulary to inform about or explain the topic.			
CC.4.W.2.e Text Types and Purposes: Provide a concluding statement or section related to the information or explanation presented.			
CC.4.W.3 Text Types and Purposes: Write narratives to develop real or imagined experiences or events using effective technique, descriptive details, and clear event sequences.			

APPENDIX: TOOL #18: THE CCSS ELA GRADES 3–8 MATRICES (FOR ALL OTHER GRADES/SUBJECTS, SEE THE DIGITAL DOWNLOAD.)

GRADE 4 ENGLISH LANGUAGE ARTS CORE STATE STANDARDS

Unpack CCSS and articulate from a student point of view. Use school data and teacher observation to add details and information regarding each standard.

CCSS	Converted/Unpacked Standard	Observations from Analysis	When in the year will this standard be covered?
CC.4.W.3.a Text Types and Purposes: Orient the reader by establishing a situation and introducing a narrator and/or characters; organize an event sequence that unfolds naturally.			
CC.4.W.3.b Text Types and Purposes: Use dialogue and description to develop experiences and events or show the responses of characters to situations.			
CC.4.W.3.c Text Types and Purposes: Use a variety of transitional words and phrases to manage the sequence of events.			
CC.4.W.3.d Text Types and Purposes: Use concrete words and phrases and sensory details to convey experiences and events precisely.			
CC.4.W.3.e Text Types and Purposes: Provide a conclusion that follows from the narrated experiences or events.			
CC.4.W.4 Production and Distribution of Writing: Produce clear and coherent writing in which the development and organization are appropriate to task, purpose, and audience. (Grade-specific expectations for writing types are defined in standards 1–3 above.)			

GRADE 4 ENGLISH LANGUAGE ARTS CORE STATE STANDARDS

Unpack CCSS and articulate from a student point of view. Use school data and teacher observation to add details and information regarding each standard.

CCSS	Converted/Unpacked Standard	Observations from Analysis	When in the year will this standard be covered?
CC.4.W.5 Production and Distribution of Writing: With guidance and support from peers and adults, develop and strengthen writing as needed by planning, revising, and editing.			
CC.4.W.6 Production and Distribution of Writing: With some guidance and support from adults, use technology, including the Internet, to produce and publish writing as well as to interact and collaborate with others; demonstrate sufficient command of keyboarding skills to type a minimum of one page in a single sitting.			
CC.4.W.7 Research to Build and Present Knowledge: Conduct short research projects that build knowledge through investigation of different aspects of a topic.			
CC.4.W.8 Research to Build and Present Knowledge: Recall relevant information from experiences or gather relevant information from print and digital sources; take notes and categorize information, and provide a list of sources.			
CC.4.W.9 Research to Build and Present Knowledge: Draw evidence from literary or informational texts to support analysis, reflection, and research.			

APPENDIX: TOOL #18: THE CCSS ELA GRADES 3–8 MATRICES (FOR ALL OTHER GRADES/SUBJECTS, SEE THE DIGITAL DOWNLOAD.)

GRADE 4 ENGLISH LANGUAGE ARTS COMMON CORE STATE STANDARDS

Unpack CCSS and articulate from a student point of view. Use school data and teacher observation to add details and information regarding each standard.

CCSS	Converted/Unpacked Standard	Observations from Analysis	When in the year will this standard be covered?
CC.4.W.9.a Research to Build and Present Knowledge: Apply *grade 4 Reading standards* to literature (e.g., "Describe in depth a character, setting, or event in a story or drama, drawing on specific details in the text [e.g., a character's thoughts, words, or actions].").			
CC.4.W.9.b Research to Build and Present Knowledge: Apply *grade 4 Reading standards* to informational texts (e.g., "Explain how an author uses reasons and evidence to support particular points in a text").			
CC.4.W.10 Range of Writing: Write routinely over extended time frames (time for research, reflection, and revision) and shorter time frames (a single sitting or a day or two) for a range of discipline-specific tasks, purposes, and audiences.			
Speaking and Listening Standards			
CC.4.SL.1 Comprehension and Collaboration: Engage effectively in a range of collaborative discussions (one-on-one, in groups, and teacher-led) with diverse partners on *grade 4 topics and texts*, building on others' ideas and expressing their own clearly.	*Example: I can participate in one-on-one and group discussions.* *I can express my ideas, and build on other people's ideas in a discussion.*		

GRADE 4 ENGLISH LANGUAGE ARTS CORE STATE STANDARDS

Unpack CCSS and articulate from a student point of view. Use school data and teacher observation to add details and information regarding each standard.

CCSS	Converted/Unpacked Standard	Observations from Analysis	When in the year will this standard be covered?
CC.4.SL.1.a Comprehension and Collaboration: Come to discussions prepared, having read or studied required material; explicitly draw on that preparation and other information known about the topic to explore ideas under discussion.			
CC.4.SL.1.b Comprehension and Collaboration: Follow agreed-upon rules for discussions and carry out assigned roles.			
CC.4.SL.1.c Comprehension and Collaboration: Pose and respond to specific questions to clarify or follow up on information, and make comments that contribute to the discussion and link to the remarks of others.			
CC.4.SL.1.d Comprehension and Collaboration: Review the key ideas expressed and explain their own ideas and understanding in light of the discussion.			
CC.4.SL.2 Comprehension and Collaboration: Paraphrase portions of a text read aloud or information presented in diverse media and formats, including visually, quantitatively, and orally.			

APPENDIX: TOOL #18: THE CCSS ELA GRADES 3–8 MATRICES (FOR ALL OTHER GRADES/SUBJECTS, SEE THE DIGITAL DOWNLOAD.)

GRADE 4 ENGLISH LANGUAGE ARTS COMMON CORE STATE STANDARDS

Unpack CCSS and articulate from a student point of view. Use school data and teacher observation to add details and information regarding each standard.

CCSS	Converted/Unpacked Standard	Observations from Analysis	When in the year will this standard be covered?
CC.4.SL.3 Comprehension and Collaboration: Identify the reasons and evidence a speaker provides to support particular points.			
CC.4.SL.4 Presentation of Knowledge and Ideas: Report on a topic or text, tell a story, or recount an experience in an organized manner, using appropriate facts and relevant, descriptive details to support main ideas or themes; speak clearly at an understandable pace.			
CC.4.SL.5 Presentation of Knowledge and Ideas: Add audio recordings and visual displays to presentations when appropriate to enhance the development of main ideas or themes.			
CC.4.SL.6 Presentation of Knowledge and Ideas: Differentiate between contexts that call for formal English (e.g., presenting ideas) and situations where informal discourse is appropriate (e.g., small-group discussion); use formal English when appropriate to task and situation.			
Language Standards			
CC.4.L.1 Conventions of Standard English: Demonstrate command of the conventions of standard English grammar and usage when writing or speaking.	*Example: I can use correct English grammar when speaking and writing.*		

GRADE 4 ENGLISH LANGUAGE ARTS CORE STATE STANDARDS

Unpack CCSS and articulate from a student point of view. Use school data and teacher observation to add details and information regarding each standard.

CCSS	Converted/Unpacked Standard	Observations from Analysis	When in the year will this standard be covered?
CC.4.L.1.a Conventions of Standard English: Use relative pronouns (*who, whose, whom, which, that*) and relative adverbs (*where, when, why*).			
CC.4.L.1.b Conventions of Standard English: Form and use the progressive (e.g., *I was walking; I am walking; I will be walking*) verb tenses.			
CC.4.L.1.c Conventions of Standard English: Use modal auxiliaries (e.g., *can, may, must*) to convey various conditions.			
CC.4.L.1.d Conventions of Standard English: Order adjectives within sentences according to conventional patterns (e.g., *a small red bag* rather than *a red small bag*).			
CC.4.L.1.e Conventions of Standard English: Form and use prepositional phrases.			
CC.4.L.1.f Conventions of Standard English: Produce complete sentences, recognizing and correcting inappropriate fragments and run-ons.			

APPENDIX: TOOL #18: THE CCSS ELA GRADES 3–8 MATRICES (FOR ALL OTHER GRADES/SUBJECTS, SEE THE DIGITAL DOWNLOAD.)

GRADE 4 ENGLISH LANGUAGE ARTS CORE STATE STANDARDS

Unpack CCSS and articulate from a student point of view. Use school data and teacher observation to add details and information regarding each standard.

CCSS	Converted/Unpacked Standard	Observations from Analysis	When in the year will this standard be covered?
CC.4.L.1.g Conventions of Standard English: Correctly use frequently confused words (e.g., *to, too, two; there, their*).			
CC.4.L.2 Conventions of Standard English: Demonstrate command of the conventions of standard English capitalization, punctuation, and spelling when writing.			
CC.4.L.2.a Conventions of Standard English: Use correct capitalization.			
CC.4.L.2.b Conventions of Standard English: Use commas and quotation marks to mark direct speech and quotations from a text.			
CC.4.L.2.c Conventions of Standard English: Use a comma before a coordinating conjunction in a compound sentence.			
CC.4.L.2.d Conventions of Standard English: Spell grade-appropriate words correctly, consulting references as needed.			

GRADE 4 ENGLISH LANGUAGE ARTS CORE STATE STANDARDS

Unpack CCSS and articulate from a student point of view. Use school data and teacher observation to add details and information regarding each standard.

CCSS	Converted/Unpacked Standard	Observations from Analysis	When in the year will this standard be covered?
CC.4.L.3 Knowledge of Language: Use knowledge of language and its conventions when writing, speaking, reading, or listening.			
CC.4.L.3.a Knowledge of Language: Choose words and phrases to convey ideas precisely.			
CC.4.L.3.b Knowledge of Language: Choose punctuation for effect.			
CC.4.L.3.c Knowledge of Language: Differentiate between contexts that call for formal English (e.g., presenting ideas) and situations where informal discourse is appropriate (e.g., small-group discussion).			
CC.4.L.4 Vocabulary Acquisition and Use: Determine or clarify the meaning of unknown and multiple-meaning words and phrases based on *grade 4 reading and content*, choosing flexibly from a range of strategies.			

APPENDIX: TOOL #18: THE CCSS ELA GRADES 3–8 MATRICES (FOR ALL OTHER GRADES/SUBJECTS, SEE THE DIGITAL DOWNLOAD.)

GRADE 4 ENGLISH LANGUAGE ARTS CORE STATE STANDARDS

Unpack CCSS and articulate from a student point of view. Use school data and teacher observation to add details and information regarding each standard.

CCSS	Converted/Unpacked Standard	Observations from Analysis	When in the year will this standard be covered?
CC.4.L.4.a Vocabulary Acquisition and Use: Use context (e.g., definitions, examples, or restatements in text) as a clue to the meaning of a word or phrase.			
CC.4.L.4.b Vocabulary Acquisition and Use: Use common, grade-appropriate Greek and Latin affixes and roots as clues to the meaning of a word (e.g., *telegraph, photograph, autograph*).			
CC.4.L.4.c Vocabulary Acquisition and Use: Consult reference materials (e.g., *dictionaries, glossaries, thesauruses*), both print and digital, to find the pronunciation and determine or clarify the precise meaning of key words and phrases.			
CC.4.L.5 Vocabulary Acquisition and Use: Demonstrate understanding of figurative language, word relationships, and nuances in word meanings.			
CC.4.L.5.a Vocabulary Acquisition and Use: Explain the meaning of simple similes and metaphors (e.g., *as pretty as a picture*) in context.			

GRADE 4 ENGLISH LANGUAGE ARTS CORE STATE STANDARDS

Unpack CCSS and articulate from a student point of view. Use school data and teacher observation to add details and information regarding each standard.

CCSS	Converted/Unpacked Standard	Observations from Analysis	When in the year will this standard be covered?
CC.4.L.5.b Vocabulary Acquisition and Use: Recognize and explain the meaning of common idioms, adages, and proverbs.			
CC.4.L.5.c Vocabulary Acquisition and Use: Demonstrate understanding of words by relating them to their opposites (antonyms) and to words with similar but not identical meanings (synonyms).			
CC.4.L.6 Vocabulary Acquisition and Use: Acquire and use accurately grade-appropriate general academic and domain-specific words and phrases, including those that signal precise actions, emotions, or states of being (e.g., *quizzed, whined, stammered*) and that are basic to a particular topic (e.g., *wildlife, conservation,* and *endangered*) when discussing animal preservation.			

APPENDIX: TOOL #18: THE CCSS ELA GRADES 3–8 MATRICES (FOR ALL OTHER GRADES/SUBJECTS, SEE THE DIGITAL DOWNLOAD.)

GRADE 5 ENGLISH LANGUAGE ARTS COMMON CORE STATE STANDARDS

Unpack CCSS and articulate from a student point of view. Use school data and teacher observation to add details and information regarding each standard.

CCSS	Converted/Unpacked Standard	Observations from Analysis	When in the year will this standard be covered?
Reading for Literature			
CC.5.R.L.1 Key Ideas and Details: Quote accurately from a text when explaining what the text says explicitly and when drawing inferences from the text.	*Example: I can quote the text to explain what it says.* I can explain what the text says directly, and what it might mean.		
CC.5.R.L.2 Key Ideas and Details: Determine a theme of a story, drama, or poem from details in the text, including how characters in a story or drama respond to challenges or how the speaker in a poem reflects upon a topic; summarize the text.			
CC.5.R.L.3 Key Ideas and Details: Compare and contrast two or more characters, settings, or events in a story or drama, drawing on specific details in the text (e.g., how characters interact).			
CC.5.R.L.4 Craft and Structure: Determine the meaning of words and phrases as they are used in a text, including figurative language such as metaphors and similes.			
CC.5.R.L.5 Craft and Structure: Explain how a series of chapters, scenes, or stanzas fits together to provide the overall structure of a particular story, drama, or poem.			
CC.5.R.L.6 Craft and Structure: Describe how a narrator's or speaker's point of view influences how events are described.			

GRADE 5 ENGLISH LANGUAGE ARTS COMMON CORE STATE STANDARDS

Unpack CCSS and articulate from a student point of view. Use school data and teacher observation to add details and information regarding each standard.

CCSS	Converted/Unpacked Standard	Observations from Analysis	When in the year will this standard be covered?
CC.5.R.L.7 Integration of Knowledge and Ideas: Analyze how visual and multimedia elements contribute to the meaning, tone, or beauty of a text (e.g., graphic novel; multimedia presentation of fiction, folktale, myth, poem).			
CC.5.R.L.9 Integration of Knowledge and Ideas: Compare and contrast stories in the same genre (e.g., mysteries and adventure stories) on their approaches to similar themes and topics.			
CC.5.R.L.10 Range of Reading and Complexity of Text: By the end of the year, read and comprehend literature, including stories, dramas, and poetry, at the high end of the grades 4–5 text complexity band independently and proficiently.			
Reading for Informational Text			
CC.5.R.I.1 Key Ideas and Details: Quote accurately from a text when explaining what the text says explicitly and when drawing inferences from the text.	*Example: I can quote the text to explain what it says.* *I can explain what the text says directly, and what it might mean.*		
CC.5.R.I.2 Key Ideas and Details: Determine two or more main ideas of a text and explain how they are supported by key details; summarize the text.			
CC.5.R.I.3 Key Ideas and Details: Explain the relationships or interactions between two or more individuals, events, ideas, or concepts in a historical, scientific, or technical text based on specific information in the text.			

APPENDIX: TOOL #18: THE CCSS ELA GRADES 3–8 MATRICES (FOR ALL OTHER GRADES/SUBJECTS, SEE THE DIGITAL DOWNLOAD.)

GRADE 5 ENGLISH LANGUAGE ARTS COMMON CORE STATE STANDARDS

Unpack CCSS and articulate from a student point of view. Use school data and teacher observation to add details and information regarding each standard.

CCSS	Converted/Unpacked Standard	Observations from Analysis	When in the year will this standard be covered?
CC.5.R.I.4 Craft and Structure: Determine the meaning of general academic and domain-specific words and phrases in a text relevant to a *grade 5 topic or subject area.*			
CC.5.R.I.5 Craft and Structure: Compare and contrast the overall structure (e.g., chronology, comparison, cause/effect, problem/ solution) of events, ideas, concepts, or information in two or more texts.			
CC.5.R.I.6 Craft and Structure: Analyze multiple accounts of the same event or topic, noting important similarities and differences in the point of view they represent.			
CC.5.R.I.7 Integration of Knowledge and Ideas: Draw on information from multiple print or digital sources, demonstrating the ability to locate an answer to a question quickly or to solve a problem efficiently.			
CC.5.R.I.8 Integration of Knowledge and Ideas: Explain how an author uses reasons and evidence to support particular points in a text, identifying which reasons and evidence support which point(s).			
CC.5.R.I.9 Integration of Knowledge and Ideas: Integrate information from several texts on the same topic in order to write or speak about the subject knowledgeably.			

GRADE 5 ENGLISH LANGUAGE ARTS COMMON CORE STATE STANDARDS

Unpack CCSS and articulate from a student point of view. Use school data and teacher observation to add details and information regarding each standard.

CCSS	Converted/Unpacked Standard	Observations from Analysis	When in the year will this standard be covered?
CC.5.R.I.10 Range of Reading and Complexity of Text: By the end of the year, read and comprehend informational texts, including history/social studies, science, and technical texts, at the high end of the grades 4–5 text complexity band independently and proficiently.			
Reading for Foundational Skills			
CC.5.R.F.3 Phonics and Word Recognition: Know and apply grade-level phonics and word analysis skills in decoding words.	*Example: I can read multisyllable words.*		
CC.5.R.F.3.a Phonics and Word Recognition: Use combined knowledge of all letter-sound correspondences, syllabication patterns, and morphology (e.g., roots and affixes) to read accurately unfamiliar multisyllabic words in context and out of context.			
CC.5.R.F.4 Fluency: Read with sufficient accuracy and fluency to support comprehension.			
CC.5.R.F.4.a Fluency: Read on-level text with purpose and understanding.			
CC.5.R.F.4.b Fluency: Read on-level prose and poetry orally with accuracy, appropriate rate, and expression on successive readings.			

APPENDIX: TOOL #18: THE CCSS ELA GRADES 3–8 MATRICES (FOR ALL OTHER GRADES/SUBJECTS, SEE THE DIGITAL DOWNLOAD.)

GRADE 5 ENGLISH LANGUAGE ARTS COMMON CORE STATE STANDARDS

Unpack CCSS and articulate from a student point of view. Use school data and teacher observation to add details and information regarding each standard.

CCSS	Converted/Unpacked Standard	Observations from Analysis	When in the year will this standard be covered?
CC.5.R.F.4.c Fluency: Use context to confirm or self-correct word recognition and understanding, rereading as necessary.			
Writing Standards			
CC.5.W.1 Text Types and Purposes: Write opinion pieces on topics or texts, supporting a point of view with reasons and information.	*Example: I can write my opinion and support it with reasons and information.*		
CC.5.W.1.a Text Types and Purposes: Introduce a topic or text clearly, state an opinion, and create an organizational structure in which ideas are logically grouped to support the writer's purpose.			
CC.5.W.1.b Text Types and Purposes: Provide logically ordered reasons that are supported by facts and details.			
CC.5.W.1.c Text Types and Purposes: Link opinion and reasons using words, phrases, and clauses (e.g., *consequently, specifically*).			
CC.5.W.1.d Text Types and Purposes: Provide a concluding statement or section related to the opinion presented.			

GRADE 5 ENGLISH LANGUAGE ARTS COMMON CORE STATE STANDARDS

Unpack CCSS and articulate from a student point of view. Use school data and teacher observation to add details and information regarding each standard.

CCSS	Converted/Unpacked Standard	Observations from Analysis	When in the year will this standard be covered?
CC.5.W.2 Text Types and Purposes: Write informative/explanatory texts to examine a topic and convey ideas and information clearly.			
CC.5.W.2.a Text Types and Purposes: Introduce a topic clearly, provide a general observation and focus, and group related information logically; include formatting (e.g., headings), illustrations, and multimedia when useful to aiding comprehension.			
CC.5.W.2.b Text Types and Purposes: Develop the topic with facts, definitions, concrete details, quotations, or other information and examples related to the topic.			
CC.5.W.2.c Text Types and Purposes: Link ideas within and across categories of information using words, phrases, and clauses (e.g., *in contrast, especially*).			
CC.5.W.2.d Text Types and Purposes: Use precise language and domain-specific vocabulary to inform about or explain the topic.			
CC.5.W.2.e Text Types and Purposes: Provide a concluding statement or section related to the information or explanation presented.			

APPENDIX: TOOL #18: THE CCSS ELA GRADES 3–8 MATRICES (FOR ALL OTHER GRADES/SUBJECTS, SEE THE DIGITAL DOWNLOAD.)

GRADE 5 ENGLISH LANGUAGE ARTS COMMON CORE STATE STANDARDS

Unpack CCSS and articulate from a student point of view. Use school data and teacher observation to add details and information regarding each standard.

CCSS	Converted/Unpacked Standard	Observations from Analysis	When in the year will this standard be covered?
CC.5.W.3 Text Types and Purposes: Write narratives to develop real or imagined experiences or events using effective technique, descriptive details, and clear event sequences.			
CC.5.W.3.a Text Types and Purposes: Orient the reader by establishing a situation and introducing a narrator and/or characters; organize an event sequence that unfolds naturally.			
CC.5.W.3.b Text Types and Purposes: Use narrative techniques, such as dialogue, description, and pacing, to develop experiences and events or show the responses of characters to situations.			
CC.5.W.3.c Text Types and Purposes: Use a variety of transitional words, phrases, and clauses to manage the sequence of events.			
CC.5.W.3.d Text Types and Purposes: Use concrete words and phrases and sensory details to convey experiences and events precisely.			
CC.5.W.3.e Text Types and Purposes: Provide a conclusion that follows from the narrated experiences or events.			

GRADE 5 ENGLISH LANGUAGE ARTS COMMON CORE STATE STANDARDS

Unpack CCSS and articulate from a student point of view. Use school data and teacher observation to add details and information regarding each standard.

CCSS	Converted/Unpacked Standard	Observations from Analysis	When in the year will this standard be covered?
CC.5.W.4 Production and Distribution of Writing: Produce clear and coherent writing in which the development and organization are appropriate to task, purpose, and audience. (Grade-specific expectations for writing types are defined in standards 1–3 above.)			
CC.5.W.5 Production and Distribution of Writing: With guidance and support from peers and adults, develop and strengthen writing as needed by planning, revising, editing, rewriting, or trying a new approach.(Editing for conventions should demonstrate command of Language standards 1–3 up to and including grade 5).			
CC.5.W.6 Production and Distribution of Writing: With some guidance and support from adults, use technology, including the Internet, to produce and publish writing as well as to interact and collaborate with others; demonstrate sufficient command of keyboarding skills to type a minimum of two pages in a single sitting.			
CC.5.W.7 Research to Build and Present Knowledge: Conduct short research projects that use several sources to build knowledge through investigation of different aspects of a topic.			
CC.5.W.8 Research to Build and Present Knowledge: Recall relevant information from experiences or gather relevant information from print and digital sources; summarize or paraphrase information in notes and finished work, and provide a list of sources.			

APPENDIX: TOOL #18: THE CCSS ELA GRADES 3–8 MATRICES (FOR ALL OTHER GRADES/SUBJECTS, SEE THE DIGITAL DOWNLOAD.)

GRADE 5 ENGLISH LANGUAGE ARTS COMMON CORE STATE STANDARDS

Unpack CCSS and articulate from a student point of view. Use school data and teacher observation to add details and information regarding each standard.

CCSS	Converted/Unpacked Standard	Observations from Analysis	When in the year will this standard be covered?
CC.5.W.9 Research to Build and Present Knowledge: Draw evidence from literary or informational texts to support analysis, reflection, and research.			
CC.5.W.9.a Research to Build and Present Knowledge: Apply *grade 5 Reading standards* to literature (e.g., "Compare and contrast two or more characters, settings, or events in a story or a drama, drawing on specific details in the text [e.g., how characters interact]").			
CC.5.W.9.b Research to Build and Present Knowledge: Apply *grade 5 Reading standards* to informational texts (e.g., "Explain how an author uses reasons and evidence to support particular points in a text, identifying which reasons and evidence support which point[s]").			
CC.5.W.10 Range of Writing: Write routinely over extended time frames (time for research, reflection, and revision) and shorter time frames (a single sitting or a day or two) for a range of discipline-specific tasks, purposes, and audiences.			
Speaking and Listening Standards			
CC.5.SL.1 Comprehension and Collaboration: Engage effectively in a range of collaborative discussions (one-on-one, in groups, and teacher-led) with diverse partners on *grade 5 topics and texts*, building on others' ideas and expressing their own clearly.	*Example: I can participate in one-on-one and group discussions.* *I can discuss my ideas, and build on other people's ideas.*		

GRADE 5 ENGLISH LANGUAGE ARTS COMMON CORE STATE STANDARDS

Unpack CCSS and articulate from a student point of view. Use school data and teacher observation to add details and information regarding each standard.

CCSS	Converted/Unpacked Standard	Observations from Analysis	When in the year will this standard be covered?
CC.5.SL.1.a Comprehension and Collaboration: Come to discussions prepared, having read or studied required material; explicitly draw on that preparation and other information known about the topic to explore ideas under discussion.			
CC.5.SL.1.b Comprehension and Collaboration: Follow agreed-upon rules for discussions and carry out assigned roles.			
CC.5.SL.1.c Comprehension and Collaboration: Pose and respond to specific questions by making comments that contribute to the discussion and elaborate on the remarks of others.			
CC.5.SL.1.d Comprehension and Collaboration: Review the key ideas expressed and draw conclusions in light of information and knowledge gained from the discussions.			
CC.5.SL.2 Comprehension and Collaboration: Summarize a text read aloud or information presented in diverse media and formats, including visually, quantitatively, and orally.			
CC.5.SL.3 Comprehension and Collaboration: Summarize the points a speaker makes and explain how each claim is supported by reasons and evidence.			

APPENDIX: TOOL #18: THE CCSS ELA GRADES 3–8 MATRICES (FOR ALL OTHER GRADES/SUBJECTS, SEE THE DIGITAL DOWNLOAD.)

GRADE 5 ENGLISH LANGUAGE ARTS COMMON CORE STATE STANDARDS

Unpack CCSS and articulate from a student point of view. Use school data and teacher observation to add details and information regarding each standard.

CCSS	Converted/Unpacked Standard	Observations from Analysis	When in the year will this standard be covered?
CC.5.SL.4 Presentation of Knowledge and Ideas: Report on a topic or text or present an opinion, sequencing ideas logically and using appropriate facts and relevant, descriptive details to support main ideas or themes; speak clearly at an understandable pace.			
CC.5.SL.5 Presentation of Knowledge and Ideas: Include multimedia components (e.g., graphics, sound) and visual displays in presentations when appropriate to enhance the development of main ideas or themes.			
CC.5.SL.6 Presentation of Knowledge and Ideas: Adapt speech to a variety of contexts and tasks, using formal English when appropriate to task and situation. (See grade 5 Language standards 1 and 3 on page 28 for specific expectations.)			
Language Standards			
CC.5.L.1 Conventions of Standard English: Demonstrate command of the conventions of standard English grammar and usage when writing or speaking.			
CC.5.L.1.a Conventions of Standard English: Explain the function of conjunctions, prepositions, and interjections in general and their function in particular sentences.	*Example: I can explain the use of conjunctions, prepositions, and interjections in general, and in specific sentences.*		
CC.5.L.1.b Conventions of Standard English: Form and use the perfect (e.g., *I had walked; I have walked; I will have walked*) verb tenses.			

GRADE 5 ENGLISH LANGUAGE ARTS COMMON CORE STATE STANDARDS

Unpack CCSS and articulate from a student point of view. Use school data and teacher observation to add details and information regarding each standard.

CCSS	Converted/Unpacked Standard	Observations from Analysis	When in the year will this standard be covered?
CC.5.L.1.c Conventions of Standard English: Use verb tense to convey various times, sequences, states, and conditions.			
CC.5.L.1.d Conventions of Standard English: Recognize and correct inappropriate shifts in verb tense.			
CC.5.L.1.e Conventions of Standard English: Use correlative conjunctions (e.g., *either/or, neither/nor*).			
CC.5.L.2 Conventions of Standard English: Demonstrate command of the conventions of standard English capitalization, punctuation, and spelling when writing.			
CC.5.L.2.a Conventions of Standard English: Use punctuation to separate items in a series.			
CC.5.L.2.b Conventions of Standard English: Use a comma to separate an introductory element from the rest of the sentence.			

APPENDIX: TOOL #18: THE CCSS ELA GRADES 3–8 MATRICES (FOR ALL OTHER GRADES/SUBJECTS, SEE THE DIGITAL DOWNLOAD.)

GRADE 5 ENGLISH LANGUAGE ARTS COMMON CORE STATE STANDARDS

Unpack CCSS and articulate from a student point of view. Use school data and teacher observation to add details and information regarding each standard.

CCSS	Converted/Unpacked Standard	Observations from Analysis	When in the year will this standard be covered?
CC.5.L.2.c Conventions of Standard English: Use a comma to set off the words yes and no (e.g., *Yes, thank you*), to set off a tag question from the rest of the sentence (e.g., *It's true, isn't it?*), and to indicate direct address (e.g., *Is that you, Steve?*).			
CC.5.L.2.d Conventions of Standard English: Use underlining, quotation marks, or italics to indicate titles of works.			
CC.5.L.2.e Conventions of Standard English: Spell grade-appropriate words correctly, consulting references as needed.			
CC.5.L.3 Knowledge of Language: Use knowledge of language and its conventions when writing, speaking, reading, or listening.			
CC.5.L.3.a Knowledge of Language: Expand, combine, and reduce sentences for meaning, reader/listener interest, and style.			
CC.5.L.3.b Knowledge of Language: Compare and contrast the varieties of English (e.g., dialects, registers) used in stories, dramas, or poems.			

GRADE 5 ENGLISH LANGUAGE ARTS COMMON CORE STATE STANDARDS

Unpack CCSS and articulate from a student point of view. Use school data and teacher observation to add details and information regarding each standard.

CCSS	Converted/Unpacked Standard	Observations from Analysis	When in the year will this standard be covered?
CC.5.L.4 Vocabulary Acquisition and Use: Determine or clarify the meaning of unknown and multiple-meaning words and phrases based on *grade 5 reading and content*, choosing flexibly from a range of strategies.			
CC.5.L.4.a Vocabulary Acquisition and Use: Use context (e.g., cause/effect relationships and comparisons in text) as a clue to the meaning of a word or phrase.			
CC.5.L.4.b Vocabulary Acquisition and Use: Use common, grade-appropriate Greek and Latin affixes and roots as clues to the meaning of a word (e.g., *photograph, photosynthesis*).			
CC.5.L.4.c Vocabulary Acquisition and Use: Consult reference materials (e.g., dictionaries, glossaries, thesauruses), both print and digital, to find the pronunciation and determine or clarify the precise meaning of key words and phrases.			
CC.5.L.5 Vocabulary Acquisition and Use: Demonstrate understanding of figurative language, word relationships, and nuances in word meanings.			
CC.5.L.5.a Vocabulary Acquisition and Use: Interpret figurative language, including similes and metaphors, in context.			

APPENDIX: TOOL #18: THE CCSS ELA GRADES 3–8 MATRICES (FOR ALL OTHER GRADES/SUBJECTS, SEE THE DIGITAL DOWNLOAD.)

GRADE 5 ENGLISH LANGUAGE ARTS COMMON CORE STATE STANDARDS

Unpack CCSS and articulate from a student point of view. Use school data and teacher observation to add details and information regarding each standard.

CCSS	Converted/Unpacked Standard	Observations from Analysis	When in the year will this standard be covered?
CC.5.L.5.b Vocabulary Acquisition and Use: Recognize and explain the meaning of common idioms, adages, and proverbs.			
CC.5.L.5.c Vocabulary Acquisition and Use: Use the relationship between particular words (e.g., synonyms, antonyms, homographs) to better understand each of the words.			
CC.5.L.6 Vocabulary Acquisition and Use: Acquire and use accurately grade-appropriate general academic and domain-specific words and phrases, including those that signal contrast, addition, and other logical relationships (e.g., *however, although, nevertheless, similarly, moreover, in addition*).			

GRADE 6 ENGLISH LANGUAGE ARTS COMMON CORE STATE STANDARD

Unpack CCSS and articulate from a student point of view. Use school data and teacher observation to add details and information regarding each standard.

CCSS	Converted/Unpacked Standard	Observations from Analysis	When in the year will this standard be covered?
Reading for Literature			
CC.6.R.L.1 Key Ideas and Details: Cite textual evidence to support analysis of what the text says explicitly as well as inferences drawn from the text.	*Example: I can locate and use evidence from a text to support a claim.* *I can distinguish between explicit and implicit meanings from text.*		
CC.6.R.L.2 Key Ideas and Details: Determine a theme or central idea of a text and how it is conveyed through particular details; provide a summary of the text distinct from personal opinions or judgments.			
CC.6.R.L.3 Key Ideas and Details: Describe how a particular story's or drama's plot unfolds in a series of episodes as well as how the characters respond or change as the plot moves toward a resolution.			
CC.6.R.L.4 Craft and Structure: Determine the meaning of words and phrases as they are used in a text, including figurative and connotative meanings; analyze the impact of a specific word choice on meaning and tone.			
CC.6.R.L.5 Craft and Structure: Analyze how a particular sentence, chapter, scene, or stanza fits into the overall structure of a text and contributes to the development of the theme, setting, or plot.			
CC.6.R.L.6 Craft and Structure: Explain how an author develops the point of view of the narrator or speaker in a text.			

APPENDIX: TOOL #18: THE CCSS ELA GRADES 3–8 MATRICES (FOR ALL OTHER GRADES/SUBJECTS, SEE THE DIGITAL DOWNLOAD.)

GRADE 6 ENGLISH LANGUAGE ARTS COMMON CORE STATE STANDARDS

Unpack CCSS and articulate from a student point of view. Use school data and teacher observation to add details and information regarding each standard.

CCSS	Converted/Unpacked Standard	Observations from Analysis	When in the year will this standard be covered?
CC.6.R.L.7 Integration of Knowledge and Ideas: Compare and contrast the experience of reading a story, drama, or poem to listening to or viewing an audio, video, or live version of the text, including contrasting what they "see" and "hear" when reading the text to what they perceive when they listen or watch.			
CC.6.R.L.9 Integration of Knowledge and Ideas: Compare and contrast texts in different forms or genres (e.g., stories and poems; historical novels and fantasy stories) in terms of their approaches to similar themes and topics.			
CC.6.R.L.10 Range of Reading and Level of Text Complexity: By the end of the year, read and comprehend literature, including stories, dramas, and poems, in the grades 6–8 text complexity band proficiently, with scaffolding as needed at the high end of the range.			
Reading for Informational Text			
CC.6.R.I.1 Key Ideas and Details: Cite textual evidence to support analysis of what the text says explicitly as well as inferences drawn from the text.	*Example: I can locate and use evidence from a text to support a claim.* *I can distinguish between explicit and implicit meanings from text.*		
CC.6.R.I.2 Key Ideas and Details: Determine a central idea of a text and how it is conveyed through particular details; provide a summary of the text distinct from personal opinions or judgments.			

GRADE 6 ENGLISH LANGUAGE ARTS COMMON CORE STATE STANDARDS

Unpack CCSS and articulate from a student point of view. Use school data and teacher observation to add details and information regarding each standard.

CCSS	Converted/Unpacked Standard	Observations from Analysis	When in the year will this standard be covered?
CC.6.R.I.3 Key Ideas and Details: Analyze in detail how a key individual, event, or idea is introduced, illustrated, and elaborated in a text (e.g., through examples or anecdotes).			
CC.6.R.I.4 Craft and Structure: Determine the meaning of words and phrases as they are used in a text, including figurative, connotative, and technical meanings.			
CC.6.R.I.5 Craft and Structure: Analyze how a particular sentence, paragraph, chapter, or section fits into the overall structure of a text and contributes to the development of the ideas.			
CC.6.R.I.6 Craft and Structure: Determine an author's point of view or purpose in a text and explain how it is conveyed in the text.			
CC.6.R.I.7 Integration of Knowledge and Ideas: Integrate information presented in different media or formats (e.g., visually, quantitatively) as well as in words to develop a coherent understanding of a topic or issue.			
CC.6.R.I.8 Integration of Knowledge and Ideas: Trace and evaluate the argument and specific claims in a text, distinguishing claims that are supported by reasons and evidence from claims that are not.			

APPENDIX: TOOL #18: THE CCSS ELA GRADES 3–8 MATRICES (FOR ALL OTHER GRADES/SUBJECTS, SEE THE DIGITAL DOWNLOAD.)

GRADE 6 ENGLISH LANGUAGE ARTS COMMON CORE STATE STANDARDS

Unpack CCSS and articulate from a student point of view. Use school data and teacher observation to add details and information regarding each standard.

CCSS	Converted/Unpacked Standard	Observations from Analysis	When in the year will this standard be covered?
CC.6.R.I.9 Integration of Knowledge and Ideas: Compare and contrast one author's presentation of events with that of another (e.g., a memoir written by and a biography on the same person).			
CC.6.R.I.10 Range of Reading and Level of Text Complexity: By the end of the year, read and comprehend literary nonfiction in the grades 6–8 text complexity band proficiently, with scaffolding as needed at the high end of the range.			
Writing Standards			
CC.6.W.1 Text Types and Purposes: Write arguments to support claims with clear reasons and relevant evidence.	*Example: I can write arguments to support claims with clear reasons and evidence.*		
CC.6.W.1.a Text Types and Purposes: Introduce claim(s) and organize the reasons and evidence clearly.			
CC.6.W.1.b Text Types and Purposes: Support claim(s) with clear reasons and relevant evidence, using credible sources and demonstrating an understanding of the topic or text.			
CC.6.W.1.c Text Types and Purposes: Use words, phrases, and clauses to clarify the relationships among claim(s) and reasons.			

GRADE 6 ENGLISH LANGUAGE ARTS COMMON CORE STATE STANDARDS

Unpack CCSS and articulate from a student point of view. Use school data and teacher observation to add details and information regarding each standard.

CCSS	Converted/Unpacked Standard	Observations from Analysis	When in the year will this standard be covered?
CC.6.W.1.d Text Types and Purposes: Establish and maintain a formal style.			
CC.6.W.1.e Text Types and Purposes: Provide a concluding statement or section that follows from the argument presented.			
CC.6.W.2 Text Types and Purposes: Write informative/explanatory texts to examine a topic and convey ideas, concepts, and information through the selection, organization, and analysis of relevant content.			
CC.6.W.2.a Text Types and Purposes: Introduce a topic; organize ideas, concepts, and information, using strategies such as definition, classification, comparison/contrast, and cause/effect; include formatting (e.g., headings), graphics (e.g., charts, tables), and multimedia when useful to aiding comprehension.			
CC.6.W.2.b Text Types and Purposes: Develop the topic with relevant facts, definitions, concrete details, quotations, or other information and examples.			
CC.6.W.2.c Text Types and Purposes: Use appropriate transitions to clarify the relationships among ideas and concepts.			

APPENDIX: TOOL #18: THE CCSS ELA GRADES 3–8 MATRICES (FOR ALL OTHER GRADES/SUBJECTS, SEE THE DIGITAL DOWNLOAD.)

GRADE 6 ENGLISH LANGUAGE ARTS COMMON CORE STATE STANDARDS

Unpack CCSS and articulate from a student point of view. Use school data and teacher observation to add details and information regarding each standard.

CCSS	Converted/Unpacked Standard	Observations from Analysis	When in the year will this standard be covered?
CC.6.W.2.d Text Types and Purposes: Use precise language and domain-specific vocabulary to inform about or explain the topic.			
CC.6.W.2.e Text Types and Purposes: Establish and maintain a formal style.			
CC.6.W.2.f Text Types and Purposes: Provide a concluding statement or section that follows from the information or explanation presented.			
CC.6.W.3 Text Types and Purposes: Write narratives to develop real or imagined experiences or events using effective technique, relevant descriptive details, and well-structured event sequences.			
CC.6.W.3.a Text Types and Purposes: Engage and orient the reader by establishing a context and introducing a narrator and/or characters; organize an event sequence that unfolds naturally and logically.			
CC.6.W.3.c Text Types and Purposes: Use a variety of transition words, phrases, and clauses to convey sequence and signal shifts from one time frame or setting to another.			

GRADE 6 ENGLISH LANGUAGE ARTS COMMON CORE STATE STANDARDS

Unpack CCSS and articulate from a student point of view. Use school data and teacher observation to add details and information regarding each standard.

CCSS	Converted/Unpacked Standard	Observations from Analysis	When in the year will this standard be covered?
CC.6.W.3.d Text Types and Purposes: Use precise words and phrases, relevant descriptive details, and sensory language to convey experiences and events.			
CC.6.W.3.e Text Types and Purposes: Provide a conclusion that follows from the narrated experiences or events.			
CC.6.W.4 Production and Distribution of Writing: Produce clear and coherent writing in which the development, organization, and style are appropriate to task, purpose, and audience. (Grade-specific expectations for writing types are defined in standards 1–3 above.)			
CC.6.W.5 Production and Distribution of Writing: With some guidance and support from peers and adults, develop and strengthen writing as needed by planning, revising, editing, rewriting, or trying a new approach. (Editing for conventions should demonstrate command of Language standards 1–3 up to and including grade 6).			
CC.6.W.6 Production and Distribution of Writing: Use technology, including the Internet, to produce and publish writing as well as to interact and collaborate with others; demonstrate sufficient command of keyboarding skills to type a minimum of three pages in a single sitting.			

APPENDIX: TOOL #18: THE CCSS ELA GRADES 3–8 MATRICES (FOR ALL OTHER GRADES/SUBJECTS, SEE THE DIGITAL DOWNLOAD.)

GRADE 6 ENGLISH LANGUAGE ARTS COMMON CORE STATE STANDARDS

Unpack CCSS and articulate from a student point of view. Use school data and teacher observation to add details and information regarding each standard.

CCSS	Converted/Unpacked Standard	Observations from Analysis	When in the year will this standard be covered?
CC.6.W.7 Research to Build and Present Knowledge: Conduct short research projects to answer a question, drawing on several sources and refocusing the inquiry when appropriate.			
CC.6.W.8 Research to Build and Present Knowledge: Gather relevant information from multiple print and digital sources; assess the credibility of each source; and quote or paraphrase the data and conclusions of others while avoiding plagiarism and providing basic bibliographic information for sources.			
CC.6.W.9 Research to Build and Present Knowledge: Draw evidence from literary or informational texts to support analysis, reflection, and research.			
CC.6.W.9.a Research to Build and Present Knowledge: Apply *grade 6 Reading standards* to literature (e.g., "Compare and contrast texts in different forms or genres [e.g., stories and poems; historical novels and fantasy stories] in terms of their approaches to similar themes and topics").			
CC.6.W.9.b Research to Build and Present Knowledge: Apply *grade 6 Reading standards* to literary nonfiction (e.g., "Trace and evaluate the argument and specific claims in a text, distinguishing claims that are supported by reasons and evidence from claims that are not").			

GRADE 6 ENGLISH LANGUAGE ARTS COMMON CORE STATE STANDARDS

Unpack CCSS and articulate from a student point of view. Use school data and teacher observation to add details and information regarding each standard.

CCSS	Converted/Unpacked Standard	Observations from Analysis	When in the year will this standard be covered?
CC.6.W.10 Range of Writing: Write routinely over extended time frames (time for research, reflection, and revision) and shorter time frames (a single sitting or a day or two) for a range of discipline-specific tasks, purposes, and audiences.			
Speaking and Listening			
CC.6.SL.1 Comprehension and Collaboration: Engage effectively in a range of collaborative discussions (one-on-one, in groups, and teacher-led) with diverse partners on *grade 6 topics, texts, and issues*, building on others' ideas and expressing their own clearly.	*Example: I can participate in one-on-one and group discussions.* *I can discuss my ideas, and build on the ideas of others in a discussion.*		
CC.6.SL.1.a Comprehension and Collaboration: Come to discussions prepared, having read or studied required material; explicitly draw on that preparation by referring to evidence on the topic, text, or issue to probe and reflect on ideas under discussion.			
CC.6.SL.1.b Comprehension and Collaboration: Follow rules for collegial discussions, set specific goals and deadlines, and define individual roles as needed.			
CC.6.SL.1.c Comprehension and Collaboration: Pose and respond to specific questions with elaboration and detail by making comments that contribute to the topic, text, or issue under discussion.			

APPENDIX: TOOL #18: THE CCSS ELA GRADES 3–8 MATRICES (FOR ALL OTHER GRADES/SUBJECTS, SEE THE DIGITAL DOWNLOAD.)

GRADE 6 ENGLISH LANGUAGE ARTS COMMON CORE STATE STANDARDS

Unpack CCSS and articulate from a student point of view Use school data and teacher observation to add details and information regarding each standard.

CCSS	Converted/Unpacked Standard	Observations from Analysis	When in the year will this standard be covered?
CC.6.SL.1.d Comprehension and Collaboration: Review the key ideas expressed and demonstrate understanding of multiple perspectives through reflection and paraphrasing.			
CC.6.SL.2 Comprehension and Collaboration: Interpret information presented in diverse media and formats (e.g., visually, quantitatively, orally) and explain how it contributes to a topic, text, or issue under study.			
CC.6.SL.3 Comprehension and Collaboration: Delineate a speaker's argument and specific claims, distinguishing claims that are supported by reasons and evidence from claims that are not.			
CC.6.SL.4 Presentation of Knowledge and Ideas: Present claims and findings, sequencing ideas logically and using pertinent descriptions, facts, and details to accentuate main ideas or themes; use appropriate eye contact, adequate volume, and clear pronunciation.			
CC.6.SL.5 Presentation of Knowledge and Ideas: Include multimedia components (e.g., graphics, images, music, sound) and visual displays in presentations to clarify information.			
CC.6.SL.6 Presentation of Knowledge and Ideas: Adapt speech to a variety of contexts and tasks, demonstrating command of formal English when indicated or appropriate.			

GRADE 6 ENGLISH LANGUAGE ARTS COMMON CORE STATE STANDARD

Unpack CCSS and articulate from a student point of view. Use school data and teacher observation to add details and information regarding each standard.

CCSS	Converted/Unpacked Standard	Observations from Analysis	When in the year will this standard be covered?
Language Standards			
CC.6.L.1 Conventions of Standard English: Demonstrate command of the conventions of standard English grammar and usage when writing or speaking.			
CC.6.L.1.a Conventions of Standard English: Ensure that pronouns are in the proper case (subjective, objective, possessive).	*Example: I can give examples of pronouns in the subjective, objective, and possessive case.*		
CC.6.L.1.b Conventions of Standard English: Use intensive pronouns (e.g., *myself, ourselves*).			
CC.6.L.1.c Conventions of Standard English: Recognize and correct inappropriate shifts in pronoun number and person.			
CC.6.L.1.d Conventions of Standard English: Recognize and correct vague pronouns (i.e., ones with unclear or ambiguous antecedents).			
CC.6.L.1.e Conventions of Standard English: Recognize variations from standard English in their own and others' writing and speaking, and identify and use strategies to improve expression in conventional language.			

APPENDIX: TOOL #18: THE CCSS ELA GRADES 3–8 MATRICES (FOR ALL OTHER GRADES/SUBJECTS, SEE THE DIGITAL DOWNLOAD.)

GRADE 6 ENGLISH LANGUAGE ARTS COMMON CORE STATE STANDARD

Unpack CCSS and articulate from a student point of view. Use school data and teacher observation to add details and information regarding each standard.

CCSS	Converted/Unpacked Standard	Observations from Analysis	When in the year will this standard be covered?
CC.6.L.2 Conventions of Standard English: Demonstrate command of the conventions of standard English capitalization, punctuation, and spelling when writing.			
CC.6.L.2.a Conventions of Standard English: Use punctuation (commas, parentheses, dashes) to set off nonrestrictive/parenthetical elements.			
CC.6.L.2.b Conventions of Standard English: Spell correctly.			
CC.6.L.3 Knowledge of Language: Use knowledge of language and its conventions when writing, speaking, reading, or listening.			
CC.6.L.3.a Knowledge of Language: Vary sentence patterns for meaning, reader/listener interest, and style.*			
CC.6.L.3.b Knowledge of Language: Maintain consistency in style and tone.*			

GRADE 6 ENGLISH LANGUAGE ARTS COMMON CORE STATE STANDARD

Unpack CCSS and articulate from a student point of view. Use school data and teacher observation to add details and information regarding each standard.

CCSS	Converted/Unpacked Standard	Observations from Analysis	When in the year will this standard be covered?
CC.6.L.4 Vocabulary Acquisition and Use: Determine or clarify the meaning of unknown and multiple-meaning words and phrases based on *grade 6 reading and content*, choosing flexibly from a range of strategies.			
CC.6.L.4.a Vocabulary Acquisition and Use: Use context (e.g., the overall meaning of a sentence or paragraph; a word's position or function in a sentence) as a clue to the meaning of a word or phrase.			
CC.6.L.4.b Vocabulary Acquisition and Use: Use common, grade-appropriate Greek or Latin affixes and roots as clues to the meaning of a word (e.g., *audience, auditory, audible*).			
CC.6.L.4.c Vocabulary Acquisition and Use: Consult reference materials (e.g., dictionaries, glossaries, thesauruses), both print and digital, to find the pronunciation of a word or determine or clarify its precise meaning or its part of speech.			
CC.6.L.4.d Vocabulary Acquisition and Use: Verify the preliminary determination of the meaning of a word or phrase (e.g., by checking the inferred meaning in context or in a dictionary).			
CC.6.L.5 Vocabulary Acquisition and Use: Demonstrate understanding of figurative language, word relationships, and nuances in word meanings.			

APPENDIX: TOOL #18: THE CCSS ELA GRADES 3–8 MATRICES (FOR ALL OTHER GRADES/SUBJECTS, SEE THE DIGITAL DOWNLOAD.)

From *Common Core State Standards for English Language Arts & Literacy in History/Social Studies, Science, and Technical Subjects*.
Copyright © 2010. National Governors Association Center for Best Practices and Council of Chief State School Officers. All rights reserved.

GRADE 6 ENGLISH LANGUAGE ARTS COMMON CORE STATE STANDARD

Unpack CCSS and articulate from a student point of view. Use school data and teacher observation to add details and information regarding each standard.

CCSS	Converted/Unpacked Standard	Observations from Analysis	When in the year will this standard be covered?
CC.6.L.5.a Vocabulary Acquisition and Use: Interpret figures of speech (e.g., personification) in context.			
CC.6.L.5.b Vocabulary Acquisition and Use: Use the relationship between particular words (e.g., cause/effect, part/whole, item/category) to better understand each of the words.			
CC.6.L.5.c Vocabulary Acquisition and Use: Distinguish among the connotations (associations) of words with similar denotations (definitions) (e.g., *stingy, scrimping, economical, unwasteful, thrifty*).			
CC.6.L.6 Vocabulary Acquisition and Use: Acquire and use accurately grade-appropriate general academic and domain-specific words and phrases; gather vocabulary knowledge when considering a word or phrase important to comprehension or expression.			

GRADE 7 ENGLISH LANGUAGE ARTS COMMON CORE STATE STANDARDS

Unpack CCSS and articulate from a student point of view. Use school data and teacher observation to add details and information regarding each standard.

CCSS	Converted/Unpacked Standard	Observations from Analysis	When in the year will this standard be covered?
Reading for Literature			
CC.7.R.L.1 Key Ideas and Details: Cite several pieces of textual evidence to support analysis of what the text says explicitly as well as inferences drawn from the text.	*Example: I can find and summarize evidence in the text to support my analysis of what it says.* *I can explain what the text says directly, and what it implies.*		
CC.7.R.L.2 Key Ideas and Details: Determine a theme or central idea of a text and analyze its development over the course of the text; provide an objective summary of the text.			
CC.7.R.L.3 Key Ideas and Details: Analyze how particular elements of a story or drama interact (e.g., how setting shapes the characters or plot).			
CC.7.R.L.4 Craft and Structure: Determine the meaning of words and phrases as they are used in a text, including figurative and connotative meanings; analyze the impact of rhymes and other repetitions of sounds (e.g., alliteration) on a specific verse or stanza of a poem or section of a story or drama.			
CC.7.R.L.5 Craft and Structure: Analyze how a drama's or poem's form or structure (e.g., soliloquy, sonnet) contributes to its meaning.			

APPENDIX: TOOL #18: THE CCSS ELA GRADES 3–8 MATRICES (FOR ALL OTHER GRADES/SUBJECTS, SEE THE DIGITAL DOWNLOAD.)

From *The Common Sense Guide to the Common Core* by Katherine McKnight, Ph.D., copyright © 2014. Free Spirit Publishing Inc., Minneapolis, MN; 800-735-7323; www.freespirit.com. This page may be reproduced for use within an individual school or district. For all other uses, contact www.freespirit.com/company/permissions.cfm.

GRADE 7 ENGLISH LANGUAGE ARTS COMMON CORE STATE STANDARDS

Unpack CCSS and articulate from a student point of view. Use school data and teacher observation to add details and information regarding each standard.

CCSS	Converted/Unpacked Standard	Observations from Analysis	When in the year will this standard be covered?
CC.7.R.L.6 Craft and Structure: Analyze how an author develops and contrasts the points of view of different characters or narrators in a text.			
CC.7.R.L.7 Integration of Knowledge and Ideas: Compare and contrast a written story, drama, or poem to its audio, filmed, staged, or multimedia version, analyzing the effects of techniques unique to each medium (e.g., lighting, sound, color, or camera focus and angles in a film).			
CC.7.R.L.9 Integration of Knowledge and Ideas: Compare and contrast a fictional portrayal of a time, place, or character and a historical account of the same period as a means of understanding how authors of fiction use or alter history.			
CC.7.R.L.10 Range of Reading and Level of Text Complexity: By the end of the year, read and comprehend literature, including stories, dramas, and poems, in the grades 6–8 text complexity band proficiently, with scaffolding as needed at the high end of the range.			
Reading for Informational Text			
CC.7.R.I.1 Key Ideas and Details: Cite several pieces of textual evidence to support analysis of what the text says explicitly as well as inferences drawn from the text.	*Example: I can use evidence from the text to support my analysis of what it says directly, and what it implies.*		

GRADE 7 ENGLISH LANGUAGE ARTS COMMON CORE STATE STANDARDS

Unpack CCSS and articulate from a student point of view. Use school data and teacher observation to add details and information regarding each standard.

CCSS	Converted/Unpacked Standard	Observations from Analysis	When in the year will this standard be covered?
CC.7.R.I.2 Key Ideas and Details: Determine two or more central ideas in a text and analyze their development over the course of the text; provide an objective summary of the text.			
CC.7.R.I.3 Key Ideas and Details: Analyze the interactions between individuals, events, and ideas in a text (e.g., how ideas influence individuals or events, or how individuals influence ideas or events).			
CC.7.R.I.4 Craft and Structure: Determine the meaning of words and phrases as they are used in a text, including figurative, connotative, and technical meanings; analyze the impact of a specific word choice on meaning and tone.			
CC.7.R.I.5 Craft and Structure: Analyze the structure an author uses to organize a text, including how the major sections contribute to the whole and to the development of the ideas.			
CC.7.R.I.6 Craft and Structure: Determine an author's point of view or purpose in a text and analyze how the author distinguishes his or her position from that of others.			
CC.7.R.I.7 Integration of Knowledge and Ideas: Compare and contrast a text to an audio, video, or multimedia version of the text, analyzing each medium's portrayal of the subject (e.g., how the delivery of a speech affects the impact of the words).			

APPENDIX: TOOL #18: THE CCSS ELA GRADES 3–8 MATRICES (FOR ALL OTHER GRADES/SUBJECTS, SEE THE DIGITAL DOWNLOAD.)

GRADE 7 ENGLISH LANGUAGE ARTS COMMON CORE STATE STANDARDS

Unpack CCSS and articulate from a student point of view. Use school data and teacher observation to add details and information regarding each standard.

CCSS	Converted/Unpacked Standard	Observations from Analysis	When in the year will this standard be covered?
CC.7.R.I.8 Integration of Knowledge and Ideas: Trace and evaluate the argument and specific claims in a text, assessing whether the reasoning is sound and the evidence is relevant and sufficient to support the claims.			
CC.7.R.I.9 Integration of Knowledge and Ideas: Analyze how two or more authors writing about the same topic shape their presentations of key information by emphasizing different evidence or advancing different interpretations of facts.			
CC.7.R.I.10 Range of Reading and Level of Text Complexity: By the end of the year, read and comprehend literary nonfiction in the grades 6–8 text complexity band proficiently, with scaffolding as needed at the high end of the range.			
Writing Standards			
CC.7.W.1 Text Types and Purposes: Write arguments to support claims with clear reasons and relevant evidence.	*Example: I can write arguments to support claims with reasons and evidence.*		
CC.7.W.1.a Text Types and Purposes: Introduce claim(s), acknowledge alternate or opposing claims, and organize the reasons and evidence logically.			
CC.7.W.1.b Text Types and Purposes: Support claim(s) with logical reasoning and relevant evidence, using accurate, credible sources and demonstrating an understanding of the topic or text.			

GRADE 7 ENGLISH LANGUAGE ARTS COMMON CORE STATE STANDARDS

Unpack CCSS and articulate from a student point of view. Use school data and teacher observation to add details and information regarding each standard.

CCSS	Converted/Unpacked Standard	Observations from Analysis	When in the year will this standard be covered?
CC.7.W.1.c Text Types and Purposes: Use words, phrases, and clauses to create cohesion and clarify the relationships among claim(s), reasons, and evidence.			
CC.7.W.1.d Text Types and Purposes: Establish and maintain a formal style.			
CC.7.W.1.e Text Types and Purposes: Provide a concluding statement or section that follows from and supports the argument presented.			
CC.7.W.2 Text Types and Purposes: Write informative/explanatory texts to examine a topic and convey ideas, concepts, and information through the selection, organization, and analysis of relevant content.			
CC.7.W.2.a Text Types and Purposes: Introduce a topic clearly, previewing what is to follow; organize ideas, concepts, and information, using strategies such as definition, classification, comparison/contrast, and cause/effect; include formatting (e.g., headings), graphics (e.g., charts, tables), and multimedia when useful to aiding comprehension.			
CC.7.W.2.b Text Types and Purposes: Develop the topic with relevant facts, definitions, concrete details, quotations, or other information and examples.			

APPENDIX: TOOL #18: THE CCSS ELA GRADES 3–8 MATRICES (FOR ALL OTHER GRADES/SUBJECTS, SEE THE DIGITAL DOWNLOAD.)

GRADE 7 ENGLISH LANGUAGE ARTS COMMON CORE STATE STANDARDS

Unpack CCSS and articulate from a student point of view. Use school data and teacher observation to add details and information regarding each standard.

CCSS	Converted/Unpacked Standard	Observations from Analysis	When in the year will this standard be covered?
CC.7.W.2.c Text Types and Purposes: Use appropriate transitions to create cohesion and clarify the relationships among ideas and concepts.			
CC.7.W.2.d Text Types and Purposes: Use precise language and domain-specific vocabulary to inform about or explain the topic.			
CC.7.W.2.e Text Types and Purposes: Establish and maintain a formal style.			
CC.7.W.2.f Text Types and Purposes: Provide a concluding statement or section that follows from and supports the information or explanation presented.			
CC.7.W.3 Text Types and Purposes: Write narratives to develop real or imagined experiences or events using effective technique, relevant descriptive details, and well-structured event sequences.			
CC.7.W.3.a Text Types and Purposes: Engage and orient the reader by establishing a context and point of view and introducing a narrator and/or characters; organize an event sequence that unfolds naturally and logically.			

GRADE 7 ENGLISH LANGUAGE ARTS COMMON CORE STATE STANDARDS

Unpack CCSS and articulate from a student point of view. Use school data and teacher observation to add details and information regarding each standard.

CCSS	Converted/Unpacked Standard	Observations from Analysis	When in the year will this standard be covered?
CC.7.W.3.b Text Types and Purposes: Use narrative techniques, such as dialogue, pacing, and description, to develop experiences, events, and/or characters.			
CC.7.W.3.c Text Types and Purposes: Use a variety of transition words, phrases, and clauses to convey sequence and signal shifts from one time frame or setting to another.			
CC.7.W.3.d Text Types and Purposes: Use precise words and phrases, relevant descriptive details, and sensory language to capture the action and convey experiences and events.			
CC.7.W.3.e Text Types and Purposes: Provide a conclusion that follows from and reflects on the narrated experiences or events.			
CC.7.W.4 Production and Distribution of Writing: Produce clear and coherent writing in which the development, organization, and style are appropriate to task, purpose, and audience. (Grade-specific expectations for writing types are defined in standards 1–3 above.)			

APPENDIX: TOOL #18: THE CCSS ELA GRADES 3–8 MATRICES (FOR ALL OTHER GRADES/SUBJECTS, SEE THE DIGITAL DOWNLOAD.)

GRADE 7 ENGLISH LANGUAGE ARTS COMMON CORE STATE STANDARDS

Unpack CCSS and articulate from a student point of view. Use school data and teacher observation to add details and information regarding each standard.

CCSS	Converted/Unpacked Standard	Observations from Analysis	When in the year will this standard be covered?
CC.7.W.5 Production and Distribution of Writing: With some guidance and support from peers and adults, develop and strengthen writing as needed by planning, revising, editing, rewriting, or trying a new approach, focusing on how well purpose and audience have been addressed. (Editing for conventions should demonstrate command of Language standards 1–3 up to and including grade 7).			
CC.7.W.6 Production and Distribution of Writing: Use technology, including the Internet, to produce and publish writing and link to and cite sources as well as to interact and collaborate with others, including linking to and citing sources.			
CC.7.W.7 Research to Build and Present Knowledge: Conduct short research projects to answer a question, drawing on several sources and generating additional related, focused questions for further research and investigation.			
CC.7.W.8 Research to Build and Present Knowledge: Gather relevant information from multiple print and digital sources, using search terms effectively; assess the credibility and accuracy of each source; and quote or paraphrase the data and conclusions of others while avoiding plagiarism and following a standard format for citation.			

GRADE 7 ENGLISH LANGUAGE ARTS COMMON CORE STATE STANDARDS

Unpack CCSS and articulate from a student point of view. Use school data and teacher observation to add details and information regarding each standard.

CCSS	Converted/Unpacked Standard	Observations from Analysis	When in the year will this standard be covered?
CC.7.W.9 Research to Build and Present Knowledge: Draw evidence from literary or informational texts to support analysis, reflection, and research.			
CC.7.W.9.a Research to Build and Present Knowledge: Apply *grade 7 Reading standards* to literature (e.g., "Compare and contrast a fictional portrayal of a time, place, or character and a historical account of the same period as a means of understanding how authors of fiction use or alter history").			
CC.7.W.9.b Research to Build and Present Knowledge: Apply *grade 7 Reading standards* to literary nonfiction (e.g. "Trace and evaluate the argument and specific claims in a text, assessing whether the reasoning is sound and the evidence is relevant and sufficient to support the claims").			
CC.7.W.10 Range of Writing: Write routinely over extended time frames (time for research, reflection, and revision) and shorter time frames (a single sitting or a day or two) for a range of discipline-specific tasks, purposes, and audiences.			
Speaking and Listening Standards			
CC.7.SL.1 Comprehension and Collaboration: Engage effectively in a range of collaborative discussions (one-on-one, in groups, and teacher-led) with diverse partners on *grade 7 topics, texts, and issues*, building on others' ideas and expressing their own clearly.	*Example: I can participate in one-on-one and group discussions.* *I can express my ideas in a discussion, and build on other people's ideas.* *I can talk about the text and other research I have done in a discussion.*		

APPENDIX: TOOL #18: THE CCSS ELA GRADES 3–8 MATRICES (FOR ALL OTHER GRADES/SUBJECTS, SEE THE DIGITAL DOWNLOAD.)

GRADE 7 ENGLISH LANGUAGE ARTS COMMON CORE STATE STANDARDS

Unpack CCSS and articulate from a student point of view. Use school data and teacher observation to add details and information regarding each standard.

CCSS	Converted/Unpacked Standard	Observations from Analysis	When in the year will this standard be covered?
CC.7.SL.1.a Comprehension and Collaboration: Come to discussions prepared, having read or researched material under study; explicitly draw on that preparation by referring to evidence on the topic, text, or issue under discussion.			
CC.7.SL.1.b Comprehension and Collaboration: Follow rules for collegial discussions, track progress toward specific goals and deadlines, and define individual roles as needed.			
CC.7.SL.1.c Comprehension and Collaboration: Pose questions that elicit elaboration and respond to others' questions and comments with relevant observations and ideas that bring the discussion back on topic as needed.			
CC.7.SL.1.d Comprehension and Collaboration: Acknowledge new information expressed by others and, when warranted, modify their own views.			
CC.7.SL.2 Comprehension and Collaboration: Analyze the main ideas and supporting details presented in diverse media and formats (e.g., visually, quantitatively, orally) and explain how the ideas clarify a topic, text, or issue under study.			
CC.7.SL.3 Comprehension and Collaboration: Delineate a speaker's argument and specific claims, evaluating the soundness of the reasoning and the relevance and sufficiency of the evidence.			

GRADE 7 ENGLISH LANGUAGE ARTS COMMON CORE STATE STANDARDS

Unpack CCSS and articulate from a student point of view. Use school data and teacher observation to add details and information regarding each standard.

CCSS	Converted/Unpacked Standard	Observations from Analysis	When in the year will this standard be covered?
CC.7.SL.4 Presentation of Knowledge and Ideas: Present claims and findings, emphasizing salient points in a focused, coherent manner with pertinent descriptions, facts, details, and examples; use appropriate eye contact, adequate volume, and clear pronunciation.			
CC.7.SL.5 Presentation of Knowledge and Ideas: Include multimedia components and visual displays in presentations to clarify claims and findings and emphasize salient points.			
CC.7.SL.6 Presentation of Knowledge and Ideas: Adapt speech to a variety of contexts and tasks, demonstrating command of formal English when indicated or appropriate.			
Language Standards			
CC.7.L.1 Conventions of Standard English: Demonstrate command of the conventions of standard English grammar and usage when writing or speaking.			
CC.7.L.1.a Conventions of Standard English: Explain the function of phrases and clauses in general and their function in specific sentences.	*Example: I can provide definitions for clauses and phrases.*		
CC.7.L.1.b Conventions of Standard English: Choose among simple, compound, complex, and compound-complex sentences to signal differing relationships among ideas.			

APPENDIX: TOOL #18: THE CCSS ELA GRADES 3–8 MATRICES (FOR ALL OTHER GRADES/SUBJECTS, SEE THE DIGITAL DOWNLOAD.)

GRADE 7 ENGLISH LANGUAGE ARTS COMMON CORE STATE STANDARDS

Unpack CCSS and articulate from a student point of view. Use school data and teacher observation to add details and information regarding each standard.

CCSS	Converted/Unpacked Standard	Observations from Analysis	When in the year will this standard be covered?
CC.7.L.1.c Conventions of Standard English: Place phrases and clauses within a sentence, recognizing and correcting misplaced and dangling modifiers.			
CC.7.L.2 Conventions of Standard English: Demonstrate command of the conventions of standard English capitalization, punctuation, and spelling when writing.			
CC.7.L.2.a Conventions of Standard English: Use a comma to separate coordinate adjectives (e.g., *It was a fascinating, enjoyable movie* but not *He wore an old[,] green shirt*).			
CC.7.L.2.b Conventions of Standard English: Spell correctly.			
CC.7.L.3 Knowledge of Language: Use knowledge of language and its conventions when writing, speaking, reading, or listening.			
CC.7.L.3.a Knowledge of Language: Choose language that expresses ideas precisely and concisely, recognizing and eliminating wordiness and redundancy.			

GRADE 7 ENGLISH LANGUAGE ARTS COMMON CORE STATE STANDARDS

Unpack CCSS and articulate from a student point of view. Use school data and teacher observation to add details and information regarding each standard.

CCSS	Converted/Unpacked Standard	Observations from Analysis	When in the year will this standard be covered?
CC.7.L.4 Vocabulary Acquisition and Use: Determine or clarify the meaning of unknown and multiple-meaning words and phrases based on *grade 7 reading and content*, choosing flexibly from a range of strategies.			
CC.7.L.4.a Vocabulary Acquisition and Use: Use context (e.g., the overall meaning of a sentence or paragraph; a word's position or function in a sentence) as a clue to the meaning of a word or phrase.			
CC.7.L.4.b Vocabulary Acquisition and Use: Use common, grade-appropriate Greek or Latin affixes and roots as clues to the meaning of a word (e.g., *belligerent, bellicose, rebel*).			
CC.7.L.4.c Vocabulary Acquisition and Use: Consult general and specialized reference materials (e.g., dictionaries, glossaries, thesauruses), both print and digital, to find the pronunciation of a word or determine or clarify its precise meaning or its part of speech.			
CC.7.L.4.d Vocabulary Acquisition and Use: Verify the preliminary determination of the meaning of a word or phrase (e.g., by checking the inferred meaning in context or in a dictionary).			

APPENDIX: TOOL #18: THE CCSS ELA GRADES 3–8 MATRICES (FOR ALL OTHER GRADES/SUBJECTS, SEE THE DIGITAL DOWNLOAD.)

GRADE 7 ENGLISH LANGUAGE ARTS COMMON CORE STATE STANDARDS

Unpack CCSS and articulate from a student point of view. Use school data and teacher observation to add details and information regarding each standard.

CCSS	Converted/Unpacked Standard	Observations from Analysis	When in the year will this standard be covered?
CC.7.L.5 Vocabulary Acquisition and Use: Demonstrate understanding of figurative language, word relationships, and nuances in word meanings.			
CC.7.L.5.a Vocabulary Acquisition and Use: Interpret figures of speech (e.g., literary, biblical, and mythological allusions) in context.			
CC.7.L.5.b Vocabulary Acquisition and Use: Use the relationship between particular words (e.g., synonym/antonym, analogy) to better understand each of the words.			
CC.7.L.5.c Vocabulary Acquisition and Use: Distinguish among the connotations (associations) of words with similar denotations (definitions) (e.g., *refined, respectful, polite, diplomatic, condescending*).			
CC.7.L.6 Vocabulary Acquisition and Use: Acquire and use accurately grade-appropriate general academic and domain-specific words and phrases; gather vocabulary knowledge when considering a word or phrase important to comprehension or expression.			

GRADE 8 ENGLISH LANGUAGE ARTS COMMON CORE STATE STANDARDS

Unpack CCSS and articulate from a student point of view. Use school data and teacher observation to add details and information regarding each standard.

CCSS	Converted/Unpacked Standard	Observations from Analysis	When in the year will this standard be covered?
Reading for Literature			
CC.8.R.L.1 Key Ideas and Details: Cite the textual evidence that most strongly supports an analysis of what the text says explicitly as well as inferences drawn from the text.	*Example: I can find and summarize evidence in the text to support my analysis of what it says.* *I can tell the difference between what the text says directly and what it implies.*		
CC.8.R.L.2 Key Ideas and Details: Determine a theme or central idea of a text and analyze its development over the course of the text, including its relationship to the characters, setting, and plot; provide an objective summary of the text.			
CC.8.R.L.3 Key Ideas and Details: Analyze how particular lines of dialogue or incidents in a story or drama propel the action, reveal aspects of a character, or provoke a decision.			
CC.8.R.L.4 Craft and Structure: Determine the meaning of words and phrases as they are used in a text, including figurative and connotative meanings; analyze the impact of specific word choices on meaning and tone, including analogies or allusions to other texts.			
CC.8.R.L.5 Craft and Structure: Compare and contrast the structure of two or more texts and analyze how the differing structure of each text contributes to its meaning and style.			

APPENDIX: TOOL #18: THE CCSS ELA GRADES 3–8 MATRICES (FOR ALL OTHER GRADES/SUBJECTS, SEE THE DIGITAL DOWNLOAD.)

GRADE 8 ENGLISH LANGUAGE ARTS COMMON CORE STATE STANDARDS

Unpack CCSS and articulate from a student point of view. Use school data and teacher observation to add details and information regarding each standard.

CCSS	Converted/Unpacked Standard	Observations from Analysis	When in the year will this standard be covered?
CC.8.R.L.6 Craft and Structure: Analyze how differences in the points of view of the characters and the audience or reader (e.g., created through the use of dramatic irony) create such effects as suspense or humor.			
CC.8.R.L.7 Integration of Knowledge and Ideas: Analyze the extent to which a filmed or live production of a story or drama stays faithful to or departs from the text or script, evaluating the choices made by the director or actors.			
CC.8.R.L.9 Integration of Knowledge and Ideas: Analyze how a modern work of fiction draws on themes, patterns of events, or character types from myths, traditional stories, or religious works such as the Bible, including describing how the material is rendered new.			
CC.8.R.L.10 Range of Reading and Level of Text Complexity: By the end of the year, read and comprehend literature, including stories, dramas, and poems, at the high end of grades 6–8 text complexity band independently and proficiently.			
Reading for Informational Text			
CC.8.R.I.1 Key Ideas and Details: Cite the textual evidence that most strongly supports an analysis of what the text says explicitly as well as inferences drawn from the text.	*Example: I can find and summarize evidence in the text to support my analysis of what it says.* I can tell the difference between what the text says directly and what it implies.		

GRADE 8 ENGLISH LANGUAGE ARTS COMMON CORE STATE STANDARDS

Unpack CCSS and articulate from a student point of view. Use school data and teacher observation to add details and information regarding each standard.

CCSS	Converted/Unpacked Standard	Observations from Analysis	When in the year will this standard be covered?
CC.8.R.I.2 Key Ideas and Details: Determine a central idea of a text and analyze its development over the course of the text, including its relationship to supporting ideas; provide an objective summary of the text.			
CC.8.R.I.3 Key Ideas and Details: Analyze how a text makes connections among and distinctions between individuals, ideas, or events (e.g., through comparisons, analogies, or categories).			
CC.8.R.I.4 Craft and Structure: Determine the meaning of words and phrases as they are used in a text, including figurative, connotative, and technical meanings; analyze the impact of specific word choices on meaning and tone, including analogies or allusions to other texts.			
CC.8.R.I.5 Craft and Structure: Analyze in detail the structure of a specific paragraph in a text, including the role of particular sentences in developing and refining a key concept.			
CC.8.R.I.6 Craft and Structure: Determine an author's point of view or purpose in a text and analyze how the author acknowledges and responds to conflicting evidence or viewpoints.			
CC.8.R.I.7 Integration of Knowledge and Ideas: Evaluate the advantages and disadvantages of using different mediums (e.g., print or digital text, video, multimedia) to present a particular topic or idea.			

APPENDIX: TOOL #18: THE CCSS ELA GRADES 3–8 MATRICES (FOR ALL OTHER GRADES/SUBJECTS, SEE THE DIGITAL DOWNLOAD.)

GRADE 8 ENGLISH LANGUAGE ARTS COMMON CORE STATE STANDARDS

Unpack CCSS and articulate from a student point of view. Use school data and teacher observation to add details and information regarding each standard.

CCSS	Converted/Unpacked Standard	Observations from Analysis	When in the year will this standard be covered?
CC.8.R.I.8 Integration of Knowledge and Ideas: Delineate and evaluate the argument and specific claims in a text, assessing whether the reasoning is sound and the evidence is relevant and sufficient; recognize when irrelevant evidence is introduced.			
CC.8.R.I.9 Integration of Knowledge and Ideas: Analyze a case in which two or more texts provide conflicting information on the same topic and identify where the texts disagree on matters of fact or interpretation.			
CC.8.R.I.10 Range of Reading and Level of Text Complexity: By the end of the year, read and comprehend literary nonfiction at the high end of the grades 6–8 text complexity band independently and proficiently.			
Writing Standards			
CC.8.W.1 Text Types and Purposes: Write arguments to support claims with clear reasons and relevant evidence.	*Example: I can write arguments to support claims with reasons and evidence.*		
CC.8.W.1.a Text Types and Purposes: Introduce claim(s), acknowledge and distinguish the claim(s) from alternate or opposing claims, and organize the reasons and evidence logically.			
CC.8.W.1.b Text Types and Purposes: Support claim(s) with logical reasoning and relevant evidence, using accurate, credible sources and demonstrating an understanding of the topic or text.			

GRADE 8 ENGLISH LANGUAGE ARTS COMMON CORE STATE STANDARDS

Unpack CCSS and articulate from a student point of view. Use school data and teacher observation to add details and information regarding each standard.

CCSS	Converted/Unpacked Standard	Observations from Analysis	When in the year will this standard be covered?
CC.8.W.1.c Text Types and Purposes: Use words, phrases, and clauses to create cohesion and clarify the relationships among claim(s), counterclaims, reasons, and evidence.			
CC.8.W.1.d Text Types and Purposes: Establish and maintain a formal style.			
CC.8.W.1.e Text Types and Purposes: Provide a concluding statement or section that follows from and supports the argument presented.			
CC.8.W.2 Text Types and Purposes: Write informative/explanatory texts to examine a topic and convey ideas, concepts, and information through the selection, organization, and analysis of relevant content.			
CC.8.W.2.a Text Types and Purposes: Introduce a topic clearly, previewing what is to follow; organize ideas, concepts, and information into broader categories; include formatting (e.g., headings), graphics (e.g., charts, tables), and multimedia when useful to aiding comprehension.			
CC.8.W.2.b Text Types and Purposes: Develop the topic with relevant, well-chosen facts, definitions, concrete details, quotations, or other information and examples.			

APPENDIX: TOOL #18: THE CCSS ELA GRADES 3–8 MATRICES (FOR ALL OTHER GRADES/SUBJECTS, SEE THE DIGITAL DOWNLOAD.)

GRADE 8 ENGLISH LANGUAGE ARTS COMMON CORE STATE STANDARDS

Unpack CCSS and articulate from a student point of view. Use school data and teacher observation to add details and information regarding each standard.

CCSS	Converted/Unpacked Standard	Observations from Analysis	When in the year will this standard be covered?
CC.8.W.2.c Text Types and Purposes: Use appropriate and varied transitions to create cohesion and clarify the relationships among ideas and concepts.			
CC.8.W.2.d Text Types and Purposes: Use precise language and domain-specific vocabulary to inform about or explain the topic.			
CC.8.W.2.e Text Types and Purposes: Establish and maintain a formal style.			
CC.8.W.2.f Text Types and Purposes: Provide a concluding statement or section that follows from and supports the information or explanation presented.			
CC.8.W.3 Text Types and Purposes: Write narratives to develop real or imagined experiences or events using effective technique, relevant descriptive details, and well-structured event sequences.			
CC.8.W.3.a Text Types and Purposes: Engage and orient the reader by establishing a context and point of view and introducing a narrator and/or characters; organize an event sequence that unfolds naturally and logically.			

GRADE 8 ENGLISH LANGUAGE ARTS COMMON CORE STATE STANDARDS

Unpack CCSS and articulate from a student point of view. Use school data and teacher observation to add details and information regarding each standard.

CCSS	Converted/Unpacked Standard	Observations from Analysis	When in the year will this standard be covered?
CC.8.W.3.b Text Types and Purposes: Use narrative techniques, such as dialogue, pacing, description, and reflection, to develop experiences, events, and/or characters.			
CC.8.W.3.c Text Types and Purposes: Use a variety of transition words, phrases, and clauses to convey sequence, signal shifts from one time frame or setting to another, and show the relationships among experiences and events.			
CC.8.W.3.d Text Types and Purposes: Use precise words and phrases, relevant descriptive details, and sensory language to capture the action and convey experiences and events.			
CC.8.W.3.e Text Types and Purposes: Provide a conclusion that follows from and reflects on the narrated experiences or events.			
CC.8.W.4 Production and Distribution of Writing: Produce clear and coherent writing in which the development, organization, and style are appropriate to task, purpose, and audience. (Grade-specific expectations for writing types are defined in standards 1–3 above.)			

APPENDIX: TOOL #18: THE CCSS ELA GRADES 3–8 MATRICES (FOR ALL OTHER GRADES/SUBJECTS, SEE THE DIGITAL DOWNLOAD.)

GRADE 8 ENGLISH LANGUAGE ARTS COMMON CORE STATE STANDARDS

Unpack CCSS and articulate from a student point of view. Use school data and teacher observation to add details and information regarding each standard.

CCSS	Converted/Unpacked Standard	Observations from Analysis	When in the year will this standard be covered?
CC.8.W.5 Production and Distribution of Writing: With some guidance and support from peers and adults, develop and strengthen writing as needed by planning, revising, editing, rewriting, or trying a new approach, focusing on how well purpose and audience have been addressed. (Editing for conventions should demonstrate command of Language standards 1–3 up to and including grade 8).			
CC.8.W.6 Production and Distribution of Writing: Use technology, including the Internet, to produce and publish writing and present the relationships between information and ideas efficiently as well as to interact and collaborate with others.			
CC.8.W.7 Research to Build and Present Knowledge: Conduct short research projects to answer a question (including a self-generated question), drawing on several sources and generating additional related, focused questions that allow for multiple avenues of exploration.			
CC.8.W.8 Research to Build and Present Knowledge: Gather relevant information from multiple print and digital sources, using search terms effectively; assess the credibility and accuracy of each source; and quote or paraphrase the data and conclusions of others while avoiding plagiarism and following a standard format for citation.			

GRADE 8 ENGLISH LANGUAGE ARTS COMMON CORE STATE STANDARDS

Unpack CCSS and articulate from a student point of view. Use school data and teacher observation to add details and information regarding each standard.

CCSS	Converted/Unpacked Standard	Observations from Analysis	When in the year will this standard be covered?
CC.8.W.9 Research to Build and Present Knowledge: Draw evidence from literary or informational texts to support analysis, reflection, and research.			
CC.8.W.9.a Research to Build and Present Knowledge: Apply *grade 8 Reading standards* to literature (e.g., "Analyze how a modern work of fiction draws on themes, patterns of events, or character types from myths, traditional stories, or religious works such as the Bible, including describing how the material is rendered new").			
CC.8.W.9.b Research to Build and Present Knowledge: Apply *grade 8 Reading standards* to literary nonfiction (e.g., "Delineate and evaluate the argument and specific claims in a text, assessing whether the reasoning is sound and the evidence is relevant and sufficient; recognize when irrelevant evidence is introduced").			
CC.8.W.10 Range of Writing: Write routinely over extended time frames (time for research, reflection, and revision) and shorter time frames (a single sitting or a day or two) for a range of discipline-specific tasks, purposes, and audiences.			

APPENDIX: TOOL #18: THE CCSS ELA GRADES 3–8 MATRICES (FOR ALL OTHER GRADES/SUBJECTS, SEE THE DIGITAL DOWNLOAD.)

GRADE 8 ENGLISH LANGUAGE ARTS COMMON CORE STATE STANDARDS

Unpack CCSS and articulate from a student point of view. Use school data and teacher observation to add details and information regarding each standard.

CCSS	Converted/Unpacked Standard	Observations from Analysis	When in the year will this standard be covered?
Speaking and Listening Standards			
CC.8.SL.1 Comprehension and Collaboration: Engage effectively in a range of collaborative discussions (one-on-one, in groups, and teacher-led) with diverse partners on grade 8 topics, texts, and issues, building on others' ideas and expressing their own clearly.	*Example: I can participate in one-on-one and group discussions.* *I can express my own ideas clearly and persuasively in a discussion.* *I can draw from and build on other people's ideas in a discussion.*		
CC.8.SL.1.a Comprehension and Collaboration: Come to discussions prepared, having read or researched material under study; explicitly draw on that preparation by referring to evidence on the topic, text, or issue to probe and reflect on ideas under discussion.			
CC.8.SL.1.b Comprehension and Collaboration: Follow rules for collegial discussions and decision-making, track progress toward specific goals and deadlines, and define individual roles as needed.			
CC.8.SL.1.c Comprehension and Collaboration: Pose questions that connect the ideas of several speakers and respond to others' questions and comments with relevant evidence, observations, and ideas.			
CC.8.SL.1.d Comprehension and Collaboration: Acknowledge new information expressed by others, and, when warranted, qualify or justify their own views in light of the evidence presented.			

GRADE 8 ENGLISH LANGUAGE ARTS COMMON CORE STATE STANDARDS

Unpack CCSS and articulate from a student point of view. Use school data and teacher observation to add details and information regarding each standard.

CCSS	Converted/Unpacked Standard	Observations from Analysis	When in the year will this standard be covered?
CC.8.SL.2 Comprehension and Collaboration: Analyze the purpose of information presented in diverse media and formats (e.g., visually, quantitatively, orally) and evaluate the motives (e.g., social, commercial, political) behind its presentation.			
CC.8.SL.3 Comprehension and Collaboration: Delineate a speaker's argument and specific claims, evaluating the soundness of the reasoning and relevance and sufficiency of the evidence and identifying when irrelevant evidence is introduced.			
CC.8.SL.4 Presentation of Knowledge and Ideas: Present claims and findings, emphasizing salient points in a focused, coherent manner with relevant evidence, sound valid reasoning, and well-chosen details; use appropriate eye contact, adequate volume, and clear pronunciation.			
CC.8.SL.5 Presentation of Knowledge and Ideas: Integrate multimedia and visual displays into presentations to clarify information, strengthen claims and evidence, and add interest.			
CC.8.SL.6 Presentation of Knowledge and Ideas: Adapt speech to a variety of contexts and tasks, demonstrating command of formal English when indicated or appropriate.			

APPENDIX: TOOL #18: THE CCSS ELA GRADES 3–8 MATRICES (FOR ALL OTHER GRADES/SUBJECTS, SEE THE DIGITAL DOWNLOAD.)

GRADE 8 ENGLISH LANGUAGE ARTS COMMON CORE STATE STANDARDS

Unpack CCSS and articulate from a student point of view. Use school data and teacher observation to add details and information regarding each standard.

CCSS	Converted/Unpacked Standard	Observations from Analysis	When in the year will this standard be covered?
CC.8.L.1 Conventions of Standard English: Demonstrate command of the conventions of standard English grammar and usage when writing or speaking.			
CC.8.L.1.a Conventions of Standard English: Explain the function of verbals (gerunds, participles, infinitives) in general and their function in particular sentences.			
CC.8.L.1.b Conventions of Standard English: Form and use verbs in the active and passive voice.			
CC.8.L.1.c Conventions of Standard English: Form and use verbs in the indicative, imperative, interrogative, conditional, and subjunctive mood.			
CC.8.L.1.d Conventions of Standard English: Recognize and correct inappropriate shifts in verb voice and mood.			
CC.8.L.2 Conventions of Standard English: Demonstrate command of the conventions of standard English capitalization, punctuation, and spelling when writing.			

GRADE 8 ENGLISH LANGUAGE ARTS COMMON CORE STATE STANDARDS

Unpack CCSS and articulate from a student point of view. Use school data and teacher observation to add details and information regarding each standard.

CCSS	Converted/Unpacked Standard	Observations from Analysis	When in the year will this standard be covered?
CC.8.L.2.a Conventions of Standard English: Use punctuation (comma, ellipsis, dash) to indicate a pause or break.			
CC.8.L.2.b Conventions of Standard English: Use an ellipsis to indicate an omission.			
CC.8.L.2.c Conventions of Standard English: Spell correctly.			
CC.8.L.3 Knowledge of Language: Use knowledge of language and its conventions when writing, speaking, reading, or listening.			
CC.8.L.3.a Knowledge of Language: Use verbs in the active and passive voice and in the conditional and subjunctive mood to achieve particular effects (e.g., emphasizing the actor or the action; expressing uncertainty or describing a state contrary to fact).			
CC.8.L.4 Vocabulary Acquisition and Use: Determine or clarify the meaning of unknown and multiple-meaning words or phrases based on grade 8 reading and content, choosing flexibly from a range of strategies.			

APPENDIX: TOOL #18: THE CCSS ELA GRADES 3–8 MATRICES (FOR ALL OTHER GRADES/SUBJECTS, SEE THE DIGITAL DOWNLOAD.)

GRADE 8 ENGLISH LANGUAGE ARTS COMMON CORE STATE STANDARDS

Unpack CCSS and articulate from a student point of view. Use school data and teacher observation to add details and information regarding each standard.

CCSS	Converted/Unpacked Standard	Observations from Analysis	When in the year will this standard be covered?
CC.8.L.4.a Vocabulary Acquisition and Use: Use context (e.g., the overall meaning of a sentence or paragraph; a word's position or function in a sentence) as a clue to the meaning of a word or phrase.			
CC.8.L.4.b Vocabulary Acquisition and Use: Use common, grade-appropriate Greek or Latin affixes and roots as clues to the meaning of a word (e.g., *precede, recede, secede*).			
CC.8.L.4.c Vocabulary Acquisition and Use: Consult general and specialized reference materials (e.g., dictionaries, glossaries, thesauruses), both print and digital, to find the pronunciation of a word or determine or clarify its precise meaning or its part of speech.			
CC.8.L.4.d Vocabulary Acquisition and Use: Verify the preliminary determination of the meaning of a word or phrase (e.g., by checking the inferred meaning in context or in a dictionary).			
CC.8.L.5 Vocabulary Acquisition and Use: Demonstrate understanding of figurative language, word relationships, and nuances in word meanings.			

GRADE 8 ENGLISH LANGUAGE ARTS COMMON CORE STATE STANDARDS

Unpack CCSS and articulate from a student point of view. Use school data and teacher observation to add details and information regarding each standard.

CCSS	Converted/Unpacked Standard	Observations from Analysis	When in the year will this standard be covered?
CC.8.L.5.a Vocabulary Acquisition and Use: Interpret figures of speech (e.g. verbal irony, puns) in context.			
CC.8.L.5.b Vocabulary Acquisition and Use: Use the relationship between particular words to better understand each of the words.			
CC.8.L.5.c Vocabulary Acquisition and Use: Distinguish among the connotations (associations) of words with similar denotations (definitions) (e.g., bullheaded, willful, firm, persistent, resolute).			
CC.8.L.6 Vocabulary Acquisition and Use: Acquire and use accurately grade-appropriate general academic and domain-specific words and phrases; gather vocabulary knowledge when considering a word or phrase important to comprehension or expression.			

APPENDIX: TOOL #18: THE CCSS ELA GRADES 3–8 MATRICES (FOR ALL OTHER GRADES/SUBJECTS, SEE THE DIGITAL DOWNLOAD.)

Index

Page references in **_bold italics_** refer to figures.

About the Author

Dr. Katherine McKnight is a recognized expert and sought-after speaker in adolescent literacy, inclusive classrooms, Common Core State Standards, and integrating technology in the twenty-first-century classroom. She began her career in education in the 1980s as a high school teacher in Chicago. Currently, as a professor of secondary education at National Louis University, Katie travels to schools and classrooms all over the United States, where she shares proven, practical models and strategies that develop the literacy skills of *all* students. Katie has published nearly a dozen books that support teaching and learning strategies that engage all learners in reading and writing for the twenty-first century. Her titles include the best-selling and award-winning *The Teacher's Big Book of Graphic Organizers*, as well as *The Second City Guide to Improv in the Classroom*, *Teaching the Classics in the Inclusive Classroom*, and *Teaching Writing in the Inclusive Classroom*. Katie has also coauthored *Methods of Teaching English in Middle and Secondary Schools*, a best-selling text in English language arts education, along with several forthcoming titles addressing the Common Core State Standards. Contact Katie at her website: **www.katherinemcknight.com**.

More Great Books from Free Spirit

RTI Success
Proven Tools and Strategies for Schools and Classrooms
by Elizabeth Whitten, Ph.D., Kelli J. Esteves, Ed.D., and Alice Woodrow, Ed.D.
256 pp.; S/C; 8½" x 11".
Digital content includes reproducibles.
For teachers and administrators, grades K–12.

Making Differentiation a Habit
How to Ensure Success in Academically Diverse Classrooms
by Diane Heacox, Ed.D.
192 pp.; S/C; 8½" x 11".
Digital content includes reproducibles.
For teachers and administrators, grades K–12.

Interested in purchasing multiple quantities and receiving volume discounts?
Contact edsales@freespirit.com or call 1.800.735.7323 and ask for Education Sales.

Many Free Spirit authors are available for speaking engagements, workshops, and keynotes.
Contact speakers@freespirit.com or call 1.800.735.7323.

For pricing information, to place an order, or to request a free catalog, contact:

Free Spirit Publishing Inc. • **217 Fifth Avenue North** • **Suite 200** • **Minneapolis, MN 55401-1299**
toll-free 800.735.7323 • **local 612.338.2068** • **fax 612.337.5050** • **help4kids@freespirit.com** • **www.freespirit.com**